ENCOUNTER

WHERE **HOPE** CAN BE **FOUND**

BILL RIESER

Published by Encounter Ministries
Versailles, KY
TheHopeEncounter.org

Editing, Cover, and Interior Design by My Writers' Connection
Cover photo by Jon Tyson

Paperback ISBN: 978-1-950714-25-4
Ebook ISBN: 978-1-950714-26-1
First Printing: March 2023

CONTENTS

Contents

A Note to the Reader

Welcome to the twelve-lesson Encounter study! When my wife, Carolynn, and I began serving in ministry, we noticed an incredible difference between people who were totally surrendered to God and His authority over their lives and people who refused to fully surrender to God in every area of their lives. We also discovered that we were nothing without Christ and that we needed to surrender everything to Him or our efforts in life and ministry would fail. We wanted Jesus to be more than our Savior; we had to make Him our LORD. We used Paul's words as the guiding verse for ministry: **"But my life is worth nothing to me unless I use it for finishing the work assigned me by the Lord Jesus—the work of telling others the Good News about the wonderful grace of God"** (Acts 20:24, NLT).

We realized that to have peace and walk in freedom, we needed to truly know God and His Word, and we should obey Him and His Word out of gratitude and love. God has been faithful to us throughout the years, and we are blessed and honored to share the vision and hope He has given us through the ministry of Encounter. God's Word is our road map. God's promises are yes and amen to those who have trusted in Jesus for the forgiveness of their sins and the gift of eternal life in Heaven—those who have chosen to follow Jesus Christ as their LORD and Savior. The only difference between us and others is God's grace. It's available for all of us, but some don't recognize that blessing. We have tasted and seen that God is good and faithful. Our Christian walk and life recovery, in our marriage and our individual lives, has been marked by believing God is who He says He is and He can do what He says He can do. We believe that. We believe in redemption and forgiveness and we have experienced the blessings of both. Hebrews 6:19, NLT, refers to the hope we have when our lives are anchored in Jesus Christ:

This **hope** is a **strong** and **trustworthy anchor for our souls**. It **leads** us through the curtain **into God's inner sanctuary**.

The twelve-lesson Encounter study is designed to help you have an Encounter with God. It is designed to help you find the hope that assures you God is faithful. We want you to know with certainty that He is a trustworthy anchor for *your* soul.

After many years of working with churches and individuals in recovery, we began to see that the brokenness of this world and the brokenness of humanity qualified every human being for recovery of some type. It is not only chemical substances from which people need recovery but life in general. We hurt other people, and other people hurt us. Those behaviors result in broken relationships and broken lives. We develop unhealthy coping mechanisms to deal with that brokenness and then take them into all of our other relationships.

Some people cope with their pain and brokenness through drugs or alcohol. They think that will numb the pain, but it only works temporarily to help them to forget. They soon realize their coping mechanism has become a cycle of dysfunction and addiction that is hurtful to themselves and others.

Other people may use different means to cope with the pain in their lives. They may not rely on chemical substances to numb the pain, but the brokenness in their lives causes them to make bad decisions or get into harmful or abusive relationships. Again, people end up getting hurt.

To reiterate, every one of us needs to recover from something or someone in life. But what does that mean, and what does life recovery look like?

A Note to the Reader

Through this Encounter study, we hope to help you see and experience what life recovery means. We didn't come up with this. God did! It's all based on God's Word. This study breaks down the message—His message—so you can easily see that God is for you and not against you. He created you. He wants to be in relationship with you. He loves you so much!

So, as you commit to this twelve-lesson study, we are praying you find the hope you are looking for. We are praying you come to know that God is bigger than any adversity you have faced, are facing, or will ever face in life. We are praying that you truly have an Encounter with God and surrender fully to His Lordship in every area of your life. We are praying that you will finally decide that it is time to get well so you can be the person God created you to be. We are praying you enjoy this great Encounter where hope can be found!

Be Blessed and Encouraged,
Bill Rieser
Encounter Pastor

WHAT IS ENCOUNTER?

Welcome! We are excited that you have decided to participate in this Encounter study.

This twelve-lesson study is designed to allow participants to have an Encounter with God. It is based on Scripture and biblical principles that help participants focus on the truth of who God is and who God says we can be "in Christ."

The truths found in God's Word can be applied to our lives to give us hope in and through (and despite) our life experiences and circumstances. God wants us to know Him, and He wants to be in relationship with us. Because of that desire, God reveals His love and plan for us through His Word.

God has given us a guidebook—the Bible. But we have to read it, believe it, and know it for it to impact our lives in a significant way. It is in knowing God and experiencing His presence that we can truly encounter Him. We can know that He is real. We can know that He loves us. We can know that God, our Father, loves us so much that He sent His son, Jesus Christ, to die for us and pay the penalty for our sins if we trust Him and follow Him. And we can know that the Holy Spirit will come and live within us to guide us in spirit and truth when we repent of our sins and ask God to forgive us and save us.

An Encounter with God doesn't have to be a one-time experience. We can encounter Him in our daily lives. That is what a relationship with God looks like. We can expect to encounter Him daily when we believe Him and seek Him in all of our ways.

The scriptures and truths in this study will help you discover how to live a life surrendered to God, a life that honors Him, a life that relies on God's faithfulness to help you every single day of your life.

We invite you to embark upon this study: *Encounter: Where Hope Can Be Found.* The Encounter study is for anyone who wants to discover true freedom and experience genuine joy and purpose in life. It truly is a study that anyone and everyone should do.

The mission of Encounter is to help **hurting** and **broken people** overcome life's adversities so they can **discover a free life devoted** to **Jesus Christ**.

ENCOUNTER'S 12 ANCHORS OF HOPE

Encounter centers around the 12 Anchors of Hope. Each lesson in this study focuses on one of these twelve anchors and includes insights and supporting scriptures. As you go through the study, you will read, pray, journal your thoughts, wait on God, and allow Him to reveal how what you have learned in this Encounter with Him can be applied to your life.

This study is designed to help you have an authentic encounter with God. With that in mind, there are two vital aspects to ensure you get the maximum benefit from this study. First, you must make the time and effort to do the work with God during the week. It's essential that you write down what you learn about yourself and what you hear from the Holy Spirit during this time. Second, we recommend that you share this written work with your Encounter study group weekly. (Because we know that some of the things you share may be very personal in nature, we suggest that groups be gender specific.) Sharing only what you've written during your private study and prayer time helps you commit to doing the work each week.

Through this study, if you decide that you want to get well and you allow God to make the necessary changes in your life to set you free, you will be changed. You will be encouraged, and you will grow in your relationship with the Lord. He will give you healing in areas that have kept you in bondage. He will transform you and you will find hope in Him!

You have the opportunity to let the Holy Spirit lead you, empower you, speak to you, give you peace, guide you into truth, and remind you that you are never alone! You are invited to go *all in* with a God who has gone all in for you! It will be a decision you won't regret.

ANCHOR 1

Decide to get well from my problems and brokenness and admit that I do a terrible job at playing God.

John 5:5-6, GNT

A man was there who had been sick for thirty-eight years. Jesus saw him lying there, and He knew that the man had been sick for such a long time; so He asked him, "Do you want to get well?"

ANCHOR 2

Believe that God's love and power can restore hope and healing.

2 Timothy 1:7, NKJV

For God has not given us a spirit of fear, but of power and of love and of a sound mind.

ANCHOR 3

Respond to the love of God by surrendering my life and will to the finished work of Jesus Christ.

Galatians 2:20, NLT

My old self has been crucified with Christ. It is no longer I who live, but Christ lives in me. So I live in this earthly body by trusting in the Son of God, who loved me and gave Himself for me.

ANCHOR 4

Trust in the power of the Holy Spirit to lead and guide me.

John 14:26, CSB

But the Counselor, the Holy Spirit, whom the Father will send in My name, will teach you all things and will remind you of everything I have said to you.

4

ANCHOR 5

Realize who I am in Christ and reject the lie that I am my character defects and sins.

2 Corinthians 5:17, NIV

Therefore, if anyone is in Christ, he is a new creation; the old has gone, the new has come!

ANCHOR 6

Get honest about my past and let the Holy Spirit reveal and rip out the root issues of my life.

Psalm 32:2, NLT

Yes, what joy for those whose record the LORD has cleared of guilt, whose lives are lived in complete honesty!

ANCHOR 7

Embrace discipleship as the pathway to transformation.

Romans 12:1-2, NIV

Therefore, I urge you, brothers and sisters, in view of God's mercy, to offer your bodies as a living sacrifice, holy and pleasing to God—this is your true and proper worship. Do not conform to the pattern of this world, but be transformed by the renewing of your mind. Then you will be able to test and approve what God's will is—his good, pleasing and perfect will.

ANCHOR 8

Choose the freedom of forgiveness to experience the healing peace of God.

Colossians 3:13-15, NLT

Make allowance for each other's faults, and forgive anyone who offends you. Remember, the Lord forgave you, so you must forgive others. Above all, clothe yourselves with love, which binds us all together in perfect harmony. And let the peace that comes from Christ rule in your hearts. For as members of one body you are called to live in peace. And always be thankful.

ANCHOR 9

Allow God's Word to become the authority over my life.

2 Timothy 3:16-17, NLT

All Scripture is inspired by God and is useful to teach us what is true and to make us realize what is wrong in our lives. It corrects us when we are wrong and teaches us to do what is right. God uses it to prepare and equip His people to do every good work.

ANCHOR 10

Commit to a daily prayer life and grow my relationship with the Father.

1 Thessalonians 5:16-18, ESV

Be joyful always; pray continually; give thanks in all circumstances, for this is God's will for you in Christ Jesus.

ANCHOR 11

Get dressed daily for battle by putting on God's armor and taking my thoughts captive.

Ephesians 6:13, NIV

Therefore put on the full armor of God, so that when the day of evil comes, you may be able to stand your ground.

6

2 Corinthians 10:4-5, NIV

The weapons we fight with are not the weapons of the world. On the contrary, they have divine power to demolish strongholds. We demolish arguments and every pretension that sets itself up against the knowledge of God, and we take captive every thought to make it obedient to Christ.

ANCHOR 12

Live out and share the hope that I now have.

1 Peter 3:15, NIV

Always be prepared to give an answer to everyone who asks you to give the reason for the hope that you have.

It's safe to say that most of us are starting this study because we want our lives to get better. We want a circumstance to change or we want to change. We may have even tried making changes before, but haven't had any success. That's because we need to allow God to make the necessary changes in our lives. Our confidence and hope cannot be in our willpower to change. Our hope has to be placed in the only One that can transform us. Only God can make those changes to surrendered hearts and lives and transform such lives.

WHERE HOPE CAN BE FOUND

As we start this Encounter Study of the 12 Anchors of Hope, it is important to understand what *hope* means.

The Greek word for *hope* is transliterated as *elpis*.
Pronounced: (el-pece')
Definition: hope, expectation, trust, confidence. It is the expectation of what is sure or certain (to anticipate, welcome).

The Hebrew word for *hope* is transliterated as *yachal*.
Pronounced: (yaw-chal')
Definition: to wait, await. It is "to wait expectantly."

In English, the word hope is a feeling of expectation and desire for a certain thing to happen or a feeling of trust. When we hope, we want something to happen or be the case. We expect or anticipate.

Encounter is described as a place "where hope can be found." As you do this study and encounter the hope, love, and presence of our Lord, do so with great anticipation and expectation that you will experience freedom and healing. Welcome the Holy Spirit to lead you as you seek Him and His truth and His presence through this study. Take your time and wait upon the Lord. Have confidence that you will find the everlasting hope of our Lord.

I encourage you to make an appointment with God every day for at least thirty minutes for the next several months to complete your work and have the best "encounter" possible.

It is not uncommon for people to feel busy, stressed out, and troubled during this study. You will most likely want to put it off or quit at some point. Please find comfort in knowing that the victory is already won and is waiting for you on the other side of completing this encounter study.

A pastor once said, "Our hope in God isn't just a wish or a dream. It's more than that. It is a sure confidence that what God says will happen." That is the same hope that we have. Our God is who He says He is, and He can do what He says He can do—and we are who He says we are, and we can do what He says we can do. Our faith is in a God we can trust, a God who is faithful, and a God who gives us the hope we need to live in freedom.

Our prayer for you as you start this journey of hope comes from **Romans 15:13, NIV:**

May the **God of hope** fill you with all joy and peace as you trust in Him, so that you may overflow with hope by the power of the **Holy Spirit**.

⚓ Anchor 1

DECIDE TO GET WELL FROM MY PROBLEMS AND BROKENNESS AND ADMIT THAT I DO A TERRIBLE JOB AT PLAYING GOD.

Pray

As you begin this lesson, pray that you will have an Encounter with God as you earnestly seek Him. Don't rush through reading everything and don't rush through praying. Take some time to stop and listen so you may hear what God wants to say to you. Be sure to write whatever comes to your mind in your journal as you use the following as a prayer to the Lord:

Lord, I want to hear Your voice—and Your voice alone—through Your Word and throughout this lesson.

With every scripture or compilation of scriptures, pray these specific prayers:

Lord, what are You saying in Your Word?
Lord, what are You saying to me?
Lord, how do You want me to apply this to my life?

Journal everything that comes to your mind.

A man was there who had been sick for thirty-eight years. Jesus saw him lying there, and He knew that the man had been sick for such a long time; so He asked him, "Do you want to get well?"

—John 5:5-6, GNT

DO YOU WANT TO GET WELL?

Read the account of Jesus healing a lame man at the pool of Bethesda.

John 5:1-15, NIV

Some time later, Jesus went up to Jerusalem for one of the Jewish festivals. Now there is in Jerusalem near the Sheep Gate a pool, which in Aramaic is called Bethesda and which is surrounded by five covered colonnades. Here a great number of disabled people used to lie—the blind, the lame, the paralyzed. One who was there had been an invalid for thirty-eight years. When Jesus saw him lying there and learned that he had been in this condition for a long time, he asked him, "Do you want to get well?"

"Sir," the invalid replied, "I have no one to help me into the pool when the water is stirred. While I am trying to get in, someone else goes down ahead of me." Then Jesus said to him, "Get up! Pick up your mat and walk." At once the man was cured; he picked up his mat and walked.

The day on which this took place was a Sabbath, and so the Jewish leaders said to the man who had been healed, "It is the Sabbath; the law forbids you to carry your mat." But he replied, "The man who made me well said to me, 'Pick up your mat and walk.'"

So they asked him, "Who is this fellow who told you to pick it up and walk?" The man who was healed had no idea who it was, for Jesus had slipped away into the crowd that was there.

10

Later Jesus found him at the temple and said to him, "See, you are well again. Stop sinning or something worse may happen to you." The man went away and told the Jewish leaders that it was Jesus who had made him well.

Focus on John 5:5-6. Jesus asked the man if he wanted to get well. At first, this may seem like a strange question. Do you think everyone is willing to admit their need for healing? Are you? What if healing requires doing something that Jesus asks? The question Jesus posed is relevant, *Do you really want to get well?* For the lame man, healing started with a decision.

The same is true for you.

Your journey starts with the decision to get well by accepting God's help. You must decide if you want to get well and allow God to bring it about in whatever way He chooses.

The twenty-eight words that Jesus spoke throughout this passage offer one of the best sermons you will ever hear:

"Do you want to get well?"

"Get up! Pick up your mat and walk."

"See, you are well again. Stop sinning or something worse may happen to you."

WHERE BROKENNESS BEGAN AND THE PROBLEM OF PLAYING GOD BEGAN

Genesis 3:1-13, NIV

Now the serpent was more crafty than any of the wild animals the Lord God had made. He said to the woman, "Did God really say, 'You must not eat from any tree in the garden'?" The woman said to the serpent, "We may eat fruit from the trees in the garden, but God did say, 'You must not eat fruit from the tree that is in the middle of the garden, and you must not touch it, or you will die.'"

"You will not certainly die," the serpent said to the woman. "For God knows that when you eat from it your eyes will be opened, and you will be like God, knowing good and evil."

When the woman saw that the fruit of the tree was good for food and pleasing to the eye, and also desirable for gaining wisdom, she took some and ate it. She also gave some to her husband, who was with her, and he ate it. Then the eyes of both of them were opened, and they realized they were naked; so they sewed fig leaves together and made coverings for themselves.

Then the man and his wife heard the sound of the Lord God as he was walking in the garden in the cool of the day, and they hid from the Lord God among the trees of the garden. But the Lord God called to the man, "Where are you?" He answered, "I heard you in the garden, and I was afraid because I was naked; so I hid." And he said, "Who told you that you were naked? Have you eaten from the tree that I commanded you not to eat from?"

The man said, "The woman you put here with me—she gave me some fruit from the tree, and I ate it." Then the Lord God said to the woman, "What is this you have done?" The woman said, "The serpent deceived me, and I ate."

12

In Genesis 3, we read that Adam and Eve sinned by trusting the word of a serpent instead of trusting God. The serpent told them they could be like God, and they believed him. The moment they exchanged the truth of God for a lie, they began worshipping the creature rather than the Creator (Romans 1:25). Their sin made them feel so ashamed that they tried to run away from God.

We inherited Adam and Eve's sinful nature. Like them, we desire to be God. When we give in to the devil's lies, we are playing God instead of believing and trusting in Him. We also tend to run from Him because of our sins.

 ## Ask Yourself

In my life, where have I tried to do God's job?

How have I sinned against Him?

How have I given in to any of the lies that the serpent presented to Eve?

How have I sinned against others?

In Psalm 32, David gets honest with God about his sin.

Psalm 32, NLT

Oh, what joy for those whose disobedience is forgiven, whose sin is put out of sight! Yes, what joy for those whose record the Lord has cleared of guilt, whose lives are lived in complete honesty!

When I refused to confess my sin, my body wasted away, and I groaned all day long. Day and night your hand of discipline was heavy on me. My strength evaporated like water in the summer heat.

Finally, I confessed all my sins to you and stopped trying to hide my guilt. I said to myself, "I will confess my rebellion to the Lord." And you forgave me! All my guilt is gone.

Therefore, let all the godly pray to you while there is still time, that they may not drown in the floodwaters of judgment. For you are my hiding place; you protect me from trouble. You surround me with songs of victory. The Lord says, "I will guide you along the best pathway for your life. I will advise you and watch over you. Do not be like a senseless horse or mule that needs a bit and bridle to keep it under control." Many sorrows come to the wicked, but unfailing love surrounds those who trust the Lord. So rejoice in the Lord and be glad, all you who obey him! Shout for joy, all you whose hearts are pure!

This psalm reveals David's acknowledgment and confession of his sin. Taking a step back to evaluate our lives can help create pathways for God to heal. Like David, we need to get real and honest about our issues.

God's first commandment is that we should have no other gods before Him (Exodus 20:3-4). In other words, we should acknowledge Him as the one true God. No person or thing should take His place of worship in our lives. When we look for answers outside of Him, we often end up making a false god or idol that will let us down (Psalm 115:4-8).

Ask Yourself

What do I need to acknowledge about myself and confess to God?

Have I made an idol out of someone or something in my life?

How have I played God by looking to others or trying to do His job?

PAUSE & PRAY

Lord, You already know everything about me. Today, I humble myself before You and ask that You reveal to me anything and everything that may be hindering me from making the decision to get well. Reveal to me the areas of my life that You want to change, heal, forgive, and set free. Reveal the areas of my life where I am playing God.

James 4:6-8, NIV

That is why Scripture says: "God opposes the proud but shows favor to the humble." Submit yourselves, then, to God. Resist the devil, and he will flee from you. Come near to God and he will come near to you. Wash your hands, you sinners, and purify your hearts, you double-minded.

1 Peter 5:6-11, NIV

Humble yourselves, therefore, under God's mighty hand, that he may lift you up in due time. Cast all your anxiety on him because he cares for you. Be alert and of sober mind. Your enemy the devil prowls around like a roaring lion looking for someone to devour. Resist him, standing firm in the faith, because you know that the family of believers throughout the world is undergoing the same kind of sufferings. And the God of all grace, who called you to his eternal glory in Christ, after you have suffered a little while, will himself restore you and make you strong, firm and steadfast. To him be the power for ever and ever. Amen.

Humility precedes blessings, renewal, and healing. Pride stops blessings, renewal, and healing. Be humble and honest. You may have been fooling yourself, but you have never fooled God. He sees your condition and He knows the truth about you. He still wants to heal you.

THE PARABLE OF THE LOST SON

Luke 15:11-24, NIV

Jesus continued: "There was a man who had two sons. The younger one said to his father, 'Father, give me my share of the estate.' So he divided his property between them. "Not long after that, the younger son got together all he had, set off for a distant country and there squandered his wealth in wild living. After he had spent everything, there was a severe famine in that whole country, and he began to be in need. So he went and hired himself out to a citizen of that country, who sent him to his fields to feed pigs. He longed to fill his stomach with the pods that the pigs were eating, but no one gave him anything.

"When he came to his senses, he said, 'How many of my father's hired servants have food to spare, and here I am starving to death! I will set out and go back to my father and say to him: Father, I have sinned against heaven and against you. I am no longer worthy to be called your son; make me like one of your hired servants.' So he got up and went to his father.

"But while he was still a long way off, his father saw him and was filled with compassion for him; he ran to his son, threw his arms around him and kissed him. "The son said to him, 'Father, I have sinned against heaven and against you. I am no longer worthy to be called your son.' "But the father said to his servants, 'Quick! Bring the best robe and put it on him. Put a ring on his finger and sandals on his feet. Bring the fattened calf and kill it. Let's have a feast and celebrate. For this son of mine was dead and is alive again; he was lost and is found.' So they began to celebrate.

The younger son was prideful and greedy in his ignorance. He thought he could control his life better than his father could. The results of his bad decisions forced him to scrounge for food among pigs. In the filth, he came to his senses. He realized that, while he was wallowing in the mud with pigs, his father's servants were living a far better life.

He humbled himself before his father, and to his great surprise, his father welcomed him home with open arms. In fact, his father saw him coming and ran to meet him. This is exactly what our Father in Heaven does for us when we come to our senses and decide that we want to get well. When we humble ourselves before Him and admit that we have messed up terribly, His response is grace and forgiveness. What great compassion our heavenly Father has for His children!

PAUSE & PRAY

Heavenly Father, today I choose to humble myself and make the decision to get well from my problems and brokenness and admit that I do a terrible job of playing God. I confess I am unable to do this without You.

 ## Ask Yourself

From what have I decided to get well?

What do Jesus's words "get up, pick up your mat, and walk" mean for me?

How have shame and guilt affected my decisions?

For what trials do I need wisdom?

Am I willing to trust God and follow His lead?

⚓ ANCHOR 2

BELIEVE THAT GOD'S LOVE AND POWER CAN RESTORE HOPE AND HEALING.

Pray

As you begin this lesson, pray that you will have an Encounter with God as you earnestly seek Him. Don't rush through reading everything and don't rush through praying. Take some time to stop and listen so you may hear what God wants to say to you. Be sure to write whatever comes to your mind in your journal as you use the following as a prayer to the Lord:

Lord, I want to hear Your voice—and Your voice alone— through Your Word and throughout this lesson.

With every scripture or compilation of scriptures, pray these specific prayers:

Lord, what are You saying in Your Word?
Lord, what are You saying to me?
Lord, how do You want me to apply this to my life?

Journal everything that comes to your mind.

For God has not given us a spirit of fear, but of power and of love and of a sound mind.
—2 Timothy 1:7, NKJV

WHAT DO YOU BELIEVE?

Believing that God's love and power can restore hope and healing, activates Anchor 2 and creates a critical crossroads where you can experience healing and growth in your life. It is here that you can choose to reconcile God's ways to your own.

 ## Ask Yourself

Do I really believe God is who He says He is?

Do I really believe God can do what He says He can do?

Do I really believe that God loves me and has my best interests at heart?

Our circumstances and the brokenness of this world can overwhelm us. Our problems can seem larger than anything else in our life. It can feel devastating when we don't have a reason to hope that things can get better for us. But when we step on the crossroad of faith, God restores our hope. Placing our faith in the right place—in God—leads us to lasting hope.

Hebrews 11:1, NIV

Now faith is being sure of what we hope for and certain of what we do not see.

Scripture is saturated with accounts of faithful people who hoped in a faithful God (Hebrews 11). God rewards those who sincerely seek Him with all their heart (Jeremiah 29:13). "And without faith, it is impossible to please God, because anyone who comes to Him must believe that He exists and that He rewards those who earnestly seek Him" (Hebrews 11:6, NIV).

Though these rewards aren't always realized in the here and now, we can set our hope fully on the grace that is yet to come (1 Peter 1:13). The heroes of faith maintained this great expectation regarding God's faithfulness. Like them, we can encounter Him as we earnestly seek Him. His presence will help us along the way and give us peace that the world cannot offer.

John 14:23-27, NIV

Jesus replied, "Anyone who loves me will obey my teaching. My Father will love them, and we will come to them and make our home with them. Anyone who does not love me will not obey my teaching. These words you hear are not my own; they belong to the Father who sent me.

"All this I have spoken while still with you. But the Advocate, the Holy Spirit, whom the Father will send in my name, will teach you all things and will remind you of everything I have said to you. Peace I leave with you; my peace I give you. I do not give to you as the world gives. Do not let your hearts be troubled and do not be afraid."

WHERE ARE YOU PLACING YOUR FAITH?

Everyone has faith. (Romans 12:3) Where they choose to place it is what makes the difference. Like the people in Hebrews 11, Christ's followers set their faith in the God of all hope. What about *your* faith? Do you have hope in God? Is your faith strong?

Our body is full of God-given muscles. For those muscles to grow and develop properly, we need to exercise them. The same holds true for our faith. While God may have given us faith, it is up to us to exercise our faith so it can grow (Philippians 2:12-13). We need to exercise our spiritual muscles so we can increase and properly develop our trust in God.

Most of us can identify times in our lives when our faith has been weak. Jesus tells us, however, that we can move mountains with faith as small as a mustard seed.

Matthew 17:14-21, NIV

When they came to the crowd, a man approached Jesus and knelt before him. "Lord, have mercy on my son," he said. "He has seizures and is suffering greatly. He often falls into the fire or into the water. I brought him to your disciples, but they could not heal him."

"You unbelieving and perverse generation," Jesus replied, "how long shall I stay with you? How long shall I put up with you? Bring the boy here to me." Jesus rebuked the demon, and it came out of the boy, and he was healed at that moment. Then the disciples came to Jesus in private and asked, "Why couldn't we drive it out?" He replied, "Because you have so little faith. Truly I tell you, if you have faith as small as a mustard seed, you can say to this mountain, 'Move from here to there,' and it will move. Nothing will be impossible for you."

Jesus was speaking to the disciples, but His words resonate with us today. We don't need huge amounts of faith to move the mountains in our lives. A little faith is a good place to start.

 ## Ask Yourself

What are the names of the mountains I want to move in my life? (Doubt, Fear, Insecurity, Addiction, Hurt, etc.)

PAUSE & PRAY

Heavenly Father, increase my faith because Your Word says it is impossible to please You without faith. I want to please You with whatever faith I have. I need faith to speak to every mountain in my life and see each one removed in Jesus's name.

HELP ME WITH MY UNBELIEF!

Mark 9:14-29, NIV

When they came to the other disciples, they saw a large crowd around them and the teachers of the law arguing with them. As soon as all the people saw Jesus, they were overwhelmed with wonder and ran to greet him. "What are you arguing with them about?" he asked.

A man in the crowd answered, "Teacher, I brought you my son, who is possessed by a spirit that has robbed him of speech. Whenever it seizes him, it throws him to the ground. He foams at the mouth, gnashes his teeth and becomes rigid. I asked your disciples to drive out the spirit, but they could not." "You unbelieving generation," Jesus replied, "how long shall I stay with you? How long shall I put up with you? Bring the boy to me." So they brought him. When the spirit saw Jesus, it immediately threw the boy into a convulsion. He fell to the ground and rolled around, foaming at the mouth. Jesus asked the boy's father, "How long has he been like this?" "From childhood," he answered. "It has often thrown him into fire or water to kill him. But if you can do anything, take pity on us and help us." "'If you can'?" said Jesus. "Everything is possible for one who believes."

Immediately the boy's father exclaimed, "I do believe; help me overcome my unbelief!" When Jesus saw that a crowd was running to the scene, he rebuked the impure spirit. "You deaf and mute spirit," he said, "I command you, come out of him and never enter him again." The spirit shrieked, convulsed him violently and came out. The boy looked so much like a corpse that many said, "He's dead." But Jesus took him by the hand and lifted him to his feet, and he stood up. After Jesus had gone indoors, his disciples asked him privately, "Why couldn't we drive it out?" He replied, "This kind can come out only by prayer."

Can you relate to the father's reply? If you still struggle with unbelief, God already knows. It's as if He is standing by, saying, "If I can?" Respond as the boy's father did and say, "Help me overcome my unbelief!"

Pause & Pray

Dear Lord, I believe but help me with my unbelief. Please reveal the areas of my life where I don't believe. Stretch my faith so that no mountain or problem can ever be bigger than You. Forgive me for telling You how big my mountains are instead of telling my mountains how big my God is!

What you believe (or do not believe) about God matters right now and for all eternity. Our faith determines how we think and act. At the end of life, most people assume that God will judge them on their actions. In reality, their legacy is determined by faith which led to their actions. It is by faith that you can encounter the love, power, hope, and peace of God.

 # Ask Yourself

What keeps me from believing that God loves me?

Whatever may hinder your belief, God wants to reassure you of His love. It is far greater than whatever problems you have in this world. He wrote a book about it. The Bible is His love story to you.

Love was God's idea. Scripture tells us that God *is* love (1 John 4:8). Sometimes, that's more easily said than believed. Thankfully, the Holy Spirit gives followers of Christ the same power and ability that Jesus promised the disciples. The Holy Spirit helps us truly experience the love of God.

Many people try to fill the void created by pain and emptiness with something other than God. They search for love in all the wrong places. Most of us have done this, in fact, and we have been hurt or we have hurt others in the process. Even so, God's love means that we have hope for redemption.

Anchor 2

Romans 5:1-8, NIV

Therefore, since we have been justified through faith, we have peace with God through our Lord Jesus Christ, through whom we have gained access by faith into this grace in which we now stand. And we boast in the hope of the glory of God. Not only so, but we also glory in our sufferings, because we know that suffering produces perseverance; perseverance, character; and character, hope. And hope does not put us to shame, because God's love has been poured out into our hearts through the Holy Spirit, who has been given to us. You see, at just the right time, when we were still powerless, Christ died for the ungodly. Very rarely will anyone die for a righteous person, though for a good person someone might possibly dare to die. But God demonstrates his own love for us in this: While we were still sinners, Christ died for us.

Ephesians 1:15-20, NIV

For this reason, ever since I heard about your faith in the Lord Jesus and your love for all God's people, I have not stopped giving thanks for you, remembering you in my prayers. I keep asking that the God of our Lord Jesus Christ, the glorious Father, may give you the Spirit of wisdom and revelation, so that you may know him better. I pray that the eyes of your heart may be enlightened in order that you may know the hope to which he has called you, the riches of his glorious inheritance in his holy people, and his incomparably great power for us who believe. That power is the same as the mighty strength he exerted when he raised Christ from the dead and seated him at his right hand in the heavenly realms,

The Apostle Paul knew that we would struggle to comprehend the love, wisdom, and power of God. This is precisely why he prayed for God to give the church spiritual wisdom—so they might grow in the knowledge of God. He wanted their hearts to be flooded with light so they could be confident in the hope God had given them.

Pause & Pray

Holy Spirit, open the eyes of my heart so that I will always be filled with the confident hope and the same power that raised Jesus Christ from the dead. Give me wisdom so that I will know You better.

It's easy to become discouraged. In our humanity, we think we must be strong in faith before we can experience the power of God. But just the opposite is true. In times of weakness, when we are at our lowest, the grace and power of God are readily available to us.

 Read, meditate, and journal the following scriptures about God's power:

Paul had begged the Lord three times to take away an infirmity. Each time the Lord gave the same response.

2 Corinthians 12:9-10, NLT

"My grace is all you need. My power works best in weakness."

Paul learned to gladly boast about his weaknesses. He understood that the power of Christ could work through him *because* of his weakness.

Philippians 4:13, NLT

For I can do everything through Christ, who gives me strength.

Paul wrote the scripture above while he was in prison. He had endured much persecution and hardship, yet his joy and confidence had grown stronger in the Lord. Christ had become everything to Paul. **Can you identify with that?**

Have you been able to find the joy of the Lord, even in your trials?

John 15:5, NIV

Jesus said, "Apart from Me you can do nothing."

Matthew 19:26, NLT

"Humanly speaking, it is impossible. But with God everything is possible."

Romans 10:17, NLT

So faith comes from hearing, that is, hearing the Good News about Christ.

Ask the Holy Spirit to restore and renew your hope as you meditate on the following:

Romans 15:4, ESV

For whatever was written in earlier times was written for our instruction, that through perseverance and the encouragement of the Scriptures we might have hope.

Romans 15:13, NKJV

Now may the God of hope fill you with all joy and peace in believing, that you may abound in hope by the power of the Holy Spirit.

Hebrews 6:19, BSB

We have this hope as an anchor for the soul, firm and secure.

Ephesians 2:12, NLT

In those days you were living apart from Christ. You were excluded from citizenship among the people of Israel, and you did not know the covenant promises God had made to them. You lived in this world without God and without hope.

Psalm 130:5, NIV

I wait for the Lord, my whole being waits, and in His word I put my hope.

Psalm 33:18, NIV

But the eyes of the LORD are on those who fear Him, on those whose hope is in his unfailing love,

Psalm 42:5, HCSB

Why am I so depressed? Why this turmoil within me? Put your hope in God, for I will still praise Him, my Savior and my God.

Romans 8:24, NIV

For in this hope we were saved. But hope that is seen is no hope at all. Who hopes for what they already have?

Romans 12:12, NIV

Be joyful in hope, patient in affliction, faithful in prayer.

Hope produces joy and perseverance as we seek the Lord. The Apostle Paul makes the case that joy and hope are our rudder through rough waters and trials. The more hope we have, the more joy we have. The more hope and joy we have, the more we will persevere as we continue to be patient in affliction and faithful in seeking the Lord in prayer.

Hebrews 10:23, NIV

Let us hold unswervingly to the hope we profess, for He who promised is faithful.

WHY SHOULD I BE AFRAID WHEN . . . ?

The Apostle Paul wrote to Timothy encouraging him to stand firm in the faith. Timothy had joined Paul's missionary journeys, which meant he faced much opposition and persecution from unbelievers. Paul wanted Timothy to remain confident in hope and faith in Christ. He knew Timothy would face hardship and trials, so he urged him to not be discouraged by fear.

Anchor 2

2 Timothy 1:3-14,NKJV

I thank God, whom I serve with a pure conscience, as my forefathers did, as without ceasing I remember you in my prayers night and day, greatly desiring to see you, being mindful of your tears, that I may be filled with joy, when I call to remembrance the genuine faith that is in you, which dwelt first in your grandmother Lois and your mother Eunice, and I am persuaded is in you also. Therefore I remind you to stir up the gift of God which is in you through the laying on of my hands. For God has not given us a spirit of fear, but of power and of love and of a sound mind.

Not Ashamed of the Gospel

Therefore do not be ashamed of the testimony of our Lord, nor of me His prisoner, but share with me in the sufferings for the gospel according to the power of God, who has saved us and called *us* with a holy calling, not according to our works, but according to His own purpose and grace which was given to us in Christ Jesus before time began, but has now been revealed by the appearing of our Savior Jesus Christ, *who* has abolished death and brought life and immortality to light through the gospel, to which I was appointed a preacher, an apostle, and a teacher of the Gentiles. For this reason I also suffer these things; nevertheless I am not ashamed, for I know whom I have believed and am persuaded that He is able to keep what I have committed to Him until that Day.

Be Loyal to the Faith

Hold fast the pattern of sound words which you have heard from me, in faith and love which are in Christ Jesus. That good thing which was committed to you, keep by the Holy Spirit who dwells in us.

Note that Paul reminds Timothy of the Holy Spirit's power within him. "For God did not give us a spirit of fear, but a spirit of power, of love and of a sound mind" (2 Timothy 1:7, NKJV).

Ask Yourself

Am I allowing fear to keep me from getting well and following God?

Do I have hope despite my trials and circumstances? Why or why not?

Do I have confidence in the power, love, and peace of God? Why or why not?

Do I believe in the saving message of Christ? Do I have a story like Paul and Timothy?

Some people don't believe God is real. You may have doubts as well. It may be difficult to believe that God can make your life better when you surrender completely to His will.

Ask Yourself

Am I afraid to go *all in* with God? If so, what's holding me back?

What are the changes I need to allow God to make in my life?

Does surrendering my will to God make me afraid of what people may think?

Paul went on to urge Timothy not to be ashamed to testify about the Lord. Much like no one can argue with how God changed Paul, neither can anyone argue with your testimony and story of how God has worked in your life. They may not readily believe Scripture or doctrine, but they can easily observe a changed life. Paul goes on to urge Timothy not to stray from sound teaching and truth and to guard it all with the help of the Holy Spirit.

30

Reflect on Paul's words to Timothy as you think about your story. Facing your fears of what happened in the past or wondering how you will resist temptations in the future can be daunting. But the same Scripture can hold true for you. The person who is following Jesus has the indwelling power of the Holy Spirit to help them in the ensuing battle. If the power of God could change Paul from a persecutor of the early church into a Christ follower, can that same power not transform each of us as well?

To believe 2 Timothy 1:7 is to be confident that believing God and following Him completely in all our ways gives us the perfect antidote to fear. God gives His followers a power they never had before, the indwelling power of the Holy Spirit. And He instills His love into believers in such a way that they can make sound and loving decisions when they rely on His guidance.

Ask Yourself

What do I believe about God and His love for me?

Why is experiencing change and living differently so scary?

What additional fears do I need God's help to overcome?

What has happened in my life that only God can restore?

On what or to whom have I fixed my hope?

Do I have a testimony of the power of God in my life? If so, what is it?

⚓
ANCHOR 3

RESPOND TO THE LOVE OF GOD BY SURRENDERING MY LIFE TO THE FINISHED WORK OF JESUS CHRIST.

Pray

As you begin this lesson, pray that you will have an Encounter with God as you earnestly seek Him. Don't rush through reading everything and don't rush through praying. Take some time to stop and listen so you may hear what God wants to say to you. Be sure to write whatever comes to your mind in your journal as you use the following as a prayer to the Lord:

Lord, I want to hear Your voice—and Your voice alone— through Your Word and throughout this lesson.

With every scripture or compilation of scriptures, pray these specific prayers:

Lord, what are You saying in Your Word?
Lord, what are You saying to me?
Lord, how do You want me to apply this to my life?

Journal everything that comes to your mind.

33

My old self has been crucified with Christ. It is no longer I who live, but Christ lives in me. So I live in this earthly body by trusting in the Son of God, who loved me and gave Himself for me.

—Galatians 2:20, NLT

HOW WILL YOU RESPOND?

We hope that at this point in your journey, you are ready to respond to the love of God.

The book of Romans is full of insight as to how the Apostle Paul instructed the Roman believers and instructs us about how we should live our lives in response to what Christ has done for us. While the writers of the Gospels (Matthew, Mark, Luke, and John) tell about the life of Jesus Christ, the writer of Romans, the Apostle Paul, tells us how significant the death of Christ (His sacrifice) is to us. For that reason, it is sometimes referred to as the gospel according to Paul. It magnifies the Good News of the Gospel and helps us to understand why we should surrender our life and will to the Lordship of Jesus Christ.

If you don't understand the finished work of Christ, you will never be compelled to live the crucified life in Christ. Read the following verses from the book of Romans to help you grasp some of this. The reading is lengthy but rich in content. These verses will give you an understanding of how seriously God views sin. It will also show you the importance of recognizing that we can never do enough in our own strength to save ourselves from our sins.

The Good News is Jesus Christ, the Son of God.

Romans 1:3-6, NLT

The Good News is about his Son. In his earthly life he was born into King David's family line, and he was shown to be the Son of God when he was raised from the dead by the power of the

Holy Spirit. He is Jesus Christ our Lord. Through Christ, God has given us the privilege and authority as apostles to tell Gentiles everywhere what God has done for them, so that they will believe and obey him, bringing glory to his name. And you are included among those Gentiles who have been called to belong to Jesus Christ.

God makes Himself known to us through His Word and creation.

Romans 1:16-20, NIV

For I am not ashamed of the gospel, because it is the power of God that brings salvation to everyone who believes: first to the Jew, then to the Gentile. For in the gospel the righteousness of God is revealed—a righteousness that is by faith from first to last, just as it is written: "The righteous will live by faith." The wrath of God is being revealed from heaven against all the godlessness and wickedness of people, who suppress the truth by their wickedness, since what may be known about God is plain to them, because God has made it plain to them. For since the creation of the world God's invisible qualities—his eternal power and divine nature—have been clearly seen, being understood from what has been made, so that people are without excuse.

We make false idols and try to play God.

Romans 1:21-25, NIV

For although they knew God, they neither glorified him as God nor gave thanks to him, but their thinking became futile and their foolish hearts were darkened. Although they claimed to be wise, they became fools and exchanged the glory of the immortal God for images made to look like a mortal human being and birds and animals and reptiles. Therefore God gave them over in the sinful desires of their hearts to sexual impurity for the degrading of their bodies with one another. They exchanged the truth about God for a lie, and worshiped and served created things rather than the Creator—who is forever praised. Amen.

Encounter

We all have a sin problem.

Romans 3:10, BSB

As it is written: "There is no one righteous, not even one."

Faith in Jesus Christ, alone, makes us righteous.

Romans 3:22-26, NIV

This righteousness is given through faith in Jesus Christ to all who believe. There is no difference between Jew and Gentile, for all have sinned and fall short of the glory of God, and all are justified freely by his grace through the redemption that came by Christ Jesus. God presented Christ as a sacrifice of atonement, through the shedding of his blood—to be received by faith. He did this to demonstrate his righteousness, because in his forbearance he had left the sins committed beforehand unpunished—he did it to demonstrate his righteousness at the present time, so as to be just and the one who justifies those who have faith in Jesus.

While we were still sinners, God sent Jesus to die for us.

Romans 5:6-8, NIV

You see, at just the right time, when we were still powerless, Christ died for the ungodly. Very rarely will anyone die for a righteous person, though for a good person someone might possibly dare to die. But God demonstrates his own love for us in this: While we were still sinners, Christ died for us.

Through Adam, we were all born into judgment and death. Through Christ, we have the opportunity to be reborn into forgiveness and life.

Roman 5:15-21, NIV

But the gift is not like the trespass. For if the many died by the trespass of the one man, how much more did God's grace and the gift that came by the grace of the one man, Jesus Christ, over-flow to the many! Nor can the gift of God be compared with

36

the result of one man's sin: The judgment followed one sin and brought condemnation, but the gift followed many trespasses and brought justification. For if, by the trespass of the one man, death reigned through that one man, how much more will those who receive God's abundant provision of grace and of the gift of righteousness reign in life through the one man, Jesus Christ!

Consequently, just as one trespass resulted in condemnation for all people, so also one righteous act resulted in justification and life for all people. For just as through the disobedience of the one man the many were made sinners, so also through the obedience of the one man the many will be made righteous.

The law was brought in so that the trespass might increase. But where sin increased, grace increased all the more, so that, just as sin reigned in death, so also grace might reign through righteousness to bring eternal life through Jesus Christ our Lord.

Sin is no longer master to the person who surrenders their life and will to Jesus Christ.

Romans 6:1-23, NIV

What shall we say, then? Shall we go on sinning so that grace may increase? By no means! We are those who have died to sin; how can we live in it any longer? Or don't you know that all of us who were baptized into Christ Jesus were baptized into his death? We were therefore buried with him through baptism into death in order that, just as Christ was raised from the dead through the glory of the Father, we too may live a new life.

For if we have been united with him in a death like his, we will certainly also be united with him in a resurrection like his. For we know that our old self was crucified with him so that the body ruled by sin might be done away with, that we should no longer be slaves to sin— because anyone who has died has been set free from sin.

Now if we died with Christ, we believe that we will also live with him. For we know that since Christ was raised from the dead, he cannot die again; death no longer has mastery over him. The death he died, he died to sin once for all; but the life he lives, he lives to God.

In the same way, count yourselves dead to sin but alive to God in Christ Jesus. Therefore do not let sin reign in your mortal body so that you obey its evil desires. Do not offer any part of yourself to sin as an instrument of wickedness, but rather offer yourselves to God as those who have been brought from death to life; and offer every part of yourself to him as an instrument of righteousness. For sin shall no longer be your master, because you are not under the law, but under grace.

What then? Shall we sin because we are not under the law but under grace? By no means! Don't you know that when you offer yourselves to someone as obedient slaves, you are slaves of the one you obey—whether you are slaves to sin, which leads to death, or to obedience, which leads to righteousness? But thanks be to God that, though you used to be slaves to sin, you have come to obey from your heart the pattern of teaching that has now claimed your allegiance. You have been set free from sin and have become slaves to righteousness.

I am using an example from everyday life because of your human limitations. Just as you used to offer yourselves as slaves to impurity and to ever-increasing wickedness, so now offer yourselves as slaves to righteousness leading to holiness. When you were slaves to sin, you were free from the control of righteousness. What benefit did you reap at that time from the things you are now ashamed of? Those things result in death!

Jesus's sacrificial death on the cross replaced the need to sacrifice innocent blood under the requirement of the Law.

Romans 8:3-4, NIV

For what the law was powerless to do because it was weakened by the flesh, God did by sending his own Son in the likeness of sinful flesh to be a sin offering. And so he condemned sin in the flesh, in order that the righteous requirement of the law might be fully met in us, who do not live according to the flesh but according to the Spirit.

If God is for us, who can be against us?

Romans 8:31, NIV

What, then, shall we say in response to these things? If God is for us, who can be against us?

Ephesians 2:1-10, NIV

As for you, you were dead in your transgressions and sins, in which you used to live when you followed the ways of this world and of the ruler of the kingdom of the air, the spirit who is now at work in those who are disobedient. All of us also lived among them at one time, gratifying the cravings of our flesh and following its desires and thoughts. Like the rest, we were by nature deserving of wrath. But because of his great love for us, God, who is rich in mercy, made us alive with Christ even when we were dead in transgressions—it is by grace you have been saved. And God raised us up with Christ and seated us with him in the heavenly realms in Christ Jesus, in order that in the coming ages he might show the incomparable riches of his grace, expressed in his kindness to us in Christ Jesus. For it is by grace you have been saved, through faith—and this is not from yourselves, it is the gift of God—not by works, so that no one can boast. For we are God's handiwork, created in Christ Jesus to do good works, which God prepared in advance for us to do.

Whether we realize it or not, we all have sinned and need a Savior. This is the bad news. But, in His great love, God brought us the Good News (the Gospel), through Jesus Christ! The only way things can be made right between God and us is through the blood of Jesus Christ. We can all choose this Good News. It is the key to understanding the love of God. He loved us so much that He provided the only acceptable sacrifice sufficient to pay for our sins.

John 10:11, NIV

"I am the good shepherd. The good shepherd lays down his life for the sheep."

John 3:16, NIV

"For God so loved the world that he gave his one and only Son, that whoever believes in him shall not perish but have eternal life."

You may recognize these verses, but have you responded to such amazing love?

Through Jesus, salvation is possible. It was a costly gift, but a gift nonetheless. Its impact changed the world forever. When we believe and receive this gift, we can be changed forever too. The beauty of God's gift of salvation is that it is for everyone. No one has gone too far, gotten too lost, or sunk too deeply into sin to become ineligible to receive the gift of salvation through Christ. When Christ became the ultimate sacrifice for all sin, He became the Good News for all who would believe.

Hebrews 10:11-18, NIV

Day after day every priest stands and performs his religious duties; again and again he offers the same sacrifices, which can never take away sins. But when this priest had offered for all time one sacrifice for sins, he sat down at the right hand of God, and since that time he waits for his enemies to be made his footstool. For by one sacrifice he has made perfect forever those who are being made holy. The Holy Spirit also testifies to us about this. First he says: "This is the covenant I will make with them after that time, says the Lord. I will put my laws in their hearts, and I will write them on their minds. Then he adds: "Their sins and lawless acts I will remember no more." And where these have been forgiven, sacrifice for sin is no longer necessary.

Righteousness is the worth of Jesus given freely to us. The shed blood of Jesus Christ transferred His righteousness onto all who would receive Him. We have no such worth and we cannot earn such value based on our own merit.

Righteousness can be a hard concept to wrap our minds around when we equate the term with our behavior. It simply means the unblemished holiness of a perfect God in every attribute. The bad news is that righteousness is not possible to attain through human effort. The standard is too high. The good news is that Jesus declares us righteous so that one day we will stand before God, and He will not see our unrighteousness but the righteousness of His Son Jesus Christ that is accredited to us when we accept what Jesus did for us on the cross.

Philippians 3:7-12, NIV

But whatever were gains to me I now consider loss for the sake of Christ. What is more, I consider everything a loss because of the surpassing worth of knowing Christ Jesus my Lord, for whose sake I have lost all things. I consider them garbage, that I may gain Christ and be found in him, not having a righteousness of my own that comes from the law, but that which is through faith in Christ—the righteousness that comes from God on the basis of faith. I want to know Christ—yes, to know the power of his resurrection and participation in his sufferings, becoming like him in his death, and so, somehow, attaining to the resurrection from the dead. Not that I have already obtained all this, or have already arrived at my goal, but I press on to take hold of that for which Christ Jesus took hold of me.

2 Corinthians 5:21, NIV

God made him who had no sin to be sin for us, so that in him we might become the righteousness of God.

God placed our sins on Jesus, who had never sinned. He also places the righteousness of Jesus on every believer who repents (or turns away from) their sin and receives (or accepts) the love of Jesus.

The reward for Jesus's righteousness is that God declares us "not guilty" of our sins and frees us of shame. The blood of Jesus gives us a clean slate. We don't have to work for such a blessing. Instead, we simply receive the gift of salvation through Jesus Christ as the blessing that allows us to live in freedom. This means that we don't have to be all cleaned up before going to God. We come to Him just as we are—muddy and dirty from our sin—and He cleans us up.

Why wouldn't everyone want to receive such a gift? Here are some possible reasons:

- They love their sins and don't want to walk away from them.

- They don't believe in Jesus Christ and don't believe He can save them.

- They have a false perception of God. They think He may be like an earthly father—maybe a punishing God, a condemning God, or a God that will leave them.

- They see people who say they are Christians living a double life or living hypocritically to what they say they believe.

- They are deceived by Satan, the god of this age. "Satan, who is the god of this world, has blinded the minds of those who don't believe. They are unable to see the glorious light of the Good News" (2 Corinthians 4:4, NLT).

- They are overwhelmed with guilt and shame and believe they don't deserve to be forgiven.

- They don't want to give up control of their own lives. Pride keeps them in denial, so they play God instead of surrendering to Him and trusting Him.

GOING ALL IN

God's free gift of salvation has both heavenly and earthly benefits for followers of Christ. It is an *all-in* plan that opens up the heavens for us to experience the abundant life that Jesus offers (John 10:10). God's desire is for us to go *all in* with Him.

John: 19:30, NIV

When he had received the drink, Jesus said, "It is finished." With that, he bowed his head and gave up his spirit.

Before Jesus died on the cross, He said, "It is finished (*Tetelestai*)." Ray Pritchard wrote the following about this wonderful Greek word:

Tetelestai comes from the verb teleo, which means "to bring to an end, to complete, to accomplish." It's a crucial word because it signifies the successful end to a particular course of action. It's the word you would use when you climb to the peak of Mt. Everest; it's the word you would use when you turn in the final copy of your dissertation; it's the word you would use when you make the final payment on your new car; it's the word you use when you cross the finish line of your first 10K run. The word means more than just "I survived." It means, "I did exactly what I set out to do."

But, there's more here than the verb itself...Tetelestai is in the perfect tense in Greek. That's significant because the perfect tense speaks of an action, which has been completed in the past with results continuing into the present. It's different from the past tense, which looks back to an event and says, "This happened." The perfect tense adds the idea that "This happened and it is still in effect today."

When Jesus cried out "It is finished," He meant, "It was finished in the past, it is still finished in the present, and it will remain finished in the future."

Note one other fact. He did not say, "I am finished," for that would imply that He died defeated and exhausted. Rather, He cried out "It is finished," meaning, "I successfully completed the work I came to do." That means He left no unfinished work behind.

43

When you accept the finished work of Christ, you realize that God forgave you of all your sins. This includes your shame and guilt. You can be free of condemnation. When you get this into your spirit, it changes everything!

The finished work of Jesus on the cross also crucified your old self and your propensity to sin. "For we know that our old self was crucified with Him so that the body ruled by sin might be done away with, that we should no longer be slaves to sin—because anyone who has died has been set free from sin" (Romans 6:6-7, NIV). The evidence that you trust in the finished work of Christ on the cross is that you have had an encounter at the cross where your old life of sin was crucified.

You crucified your past.

You crucified your desire to control other people.

You crucified your shame and guilt.

You crucified your pain, addiction, and character defects.

You crucified your anger, lust, disorders, and co-dependencies.

You crucified your bitterness, unforgiveness, and fear.

You crucified your old life.

Believe by faith that all of those things were nailed to the cross and buried in the grave. The only thing that came back to life is Christ in you.

The finished work of Christ compels me to live the crucified life of Christ.

Philippians 1:21, NIV

For to me, to live is Christ and to die is gain.

The remaining Anchors of Hope will have no impact unless you trust in the finished work of Christ. The key to living in freedom is trusting in the finished work of Christ. Everyone trusts something or someone. You either trust in the finished work of Christ, or you trust in yourself. When you don't trust in Christ, you will try to accomplish things in your own strength and fail every time.

Galatians 2:20, NLT

My old self has been crucified with Christ. It is no longer I who live, but Christ lives in me. So I live in this earthly body by trusting in the Son of God, who loved me and gave Himself for me.

If we trust in Christ, we begin to live a life that resembles Galatians 2:20—a life of gratitude for what Jesus has done for us. We cannot work to earn something Jesus has already given us. Neither should we use that gift of grace as an excuse to keep living in sin. We can only truly experience freedom and the life of Christ when we receive the gift of salvation and die daily to our selfishness and our sinful nature.

To recap, the story of God and man can be summed up like this: God is love and His love is pure and holy. God made us in His image. Adam and Eve sinned and it ruined everything. We inherited that sin and live in a broken world. Because God is holy, He cannot be in the presence of sin. Therefore, sin separated us from our loving God and gave us a death sentence that declares us guilty. We were incapable of fixing our sin problem and separation from God.

Separation from those you love the most will make you do outrageous and radical things. Our Father did just that. He came up with the greatest plan ever:

- A plan that would restore our relationship with God and bridge the gap back to Him.
- A plan that would forgive anyone for all their sins so they could have a permanent residence in Heaven for eternity.
- A plan that is free to us but cost God *everything*. He sacrificed His one and only Son as payment for our sins.
- A plan that solved our sin problem when God's Son, Jesus Christ, took on our sins, became our sins, died for our sins, and defeated our sins on the cross and from the grave.

He did that for us! He did that for you! What is your response to this outrageous act of unprecedented love?

PAUSE & PRAY

If you have never received Jesus Christ as your Lord and Savior, you can today. If you are unsure of how to do that, you can say this prayer out loud to God:

Father, I am a sinner. I have sinned against You and others. I repent of my sins and turn from my sins. I trust in Jesus Christ for the forgiveness of my sins and for the free gift of eternal life. I believe that Jesus is the Christ, the Son of God. I believe that He died for my sins and rose from the dead so I can live with Him forever in Heaven and for Him here on earth. I acknowledge Jesus as my Savior and my Lord. It is my desire to love Him back by fully devoting my life to Him. Fill me with Your Holy Spirit so I will have the power and grace to live the life You planned for me. Thank You for loving and forgiving me. Thank You for welcoming me into Your family and making me a child of the one true King.

If you just prayed this prayer, welcome to the Kingdom of Heaven!

 ## Ask Yourself

How have I responded to the love of God? Is anything keeping me from receiving His gift?

What part of my past and present have I not crucified with Christ and surrendered to His Lordship?

In what ways have I recognized that I am not trusting in the finished work of Christ?

⚓ Anchor 4

TRUST IN THE POWER OF THE HOLY SPIRIT TO LEAD AND GUIDE ME.

Pray

As you begin this lesson, pray that you will have an Encounter with God as you earnestly seek Him. Don't rush through reading everything and don't rush through praying. Take some time to stop and listen so you may hear what God wants to say to you. Be sure to write whatever comes to your mind in your journal as you use the following as a prayer to the Lord:

Lord, I want to hear Your voice—and Your voice alone—through Your Word and throughout this lesson.

With every scripture or compilation of scriptures, pray these specific prayers:

Lord, what are You saying in Your Word?
Lord, what are You saying to me?
Lord, how do You want me to apply this to my life?

Journal everything that comes to your mind.

"But the Counselor, the Holy Spirit, whom the Father will send in my name, will teach you all things and will remind you of everything I have said to you."

—John 14:26, CSB

LIVING WITH THE HOLY SPIRIT

When you become a follower of Jesus, you are not left alone. From the beginning, God had a plan to save you and be with you every step of the way.

The Holy Spirit is vital to your Christian walk. He is your Counselor, Guide, Comforter, Companion, Helper, and source of Power. He does all this and more to help you live the Christian life. You cannot do it in your own power.

God, the Father, and Jesus, the Son, are both in Heaven. The Holy Spirit is the only member of the Trinity that is with believers here on earth. He lives within followers of Christ. Knowing Him and following Him is the difference between having a victorious life or a defeated one.

The Holy Spirit is the greatest power in the universe, and He lives within the hearts of every Christ follower. If you don't give Him full operating room to work in your life, you'll have limited power. But, if you give the Holy Spirit full reign and complete power in your life, you are a force to be reckoned with. A person totally yielded to and guided by the Holy Spirit is filled with the same power that raised Jesus Christ from the dead! God wants you to know that truth and live like you believe it.

It is important to search God's Word in all matters, but particularly when it comes to learning who the Holy Spirit is. The scriptures below will help guide you to knowing Him more:

The Holy Spirit is a person of the Trinity.

Matthew 3:16, NIV

As soon as Jesus was baptized, he went up out of the water. At that moment heaven was opened, and he saw the Spirit of God descending like a dove and alighting on him.

The Holy Spirit is everywhere. You cannot escape His presence.

Psalm 139:7-8, NIV

Where can I go from your Spirit? Where can I flee from your presence?

If I go up to the heavens, you are there; if I make my bed in the depths, you are there.

The Holy Spirit is your Counselor who lives inside of you.

John 14:16-17, NIV

"And I will ask the Father, and he will give you another advocate to help you and be with you forever— the Spirit of truth. The world cannot accept him, because it neither sees him nor knows him. But you know him, for he lives with you and will be in you."

John 16:7, NIV

"But very truly I tell you, it is for your good that I am going away. Unless I go away, the Advocate will not come to you; but if I go, I will send him to you."

The Holy Spirit is a teacher.

John 14:26, NIV

"But the Advocate, the Holy Spirit, whom the Father will send in my name, will teach you all things and will remind you of everything I have said to you."

The Holy Spirit testifies and equips.

John 15:26, NIV

"When the Advocate comes, whom I will send to you from the Father—the Spirit of truth who goes out from the Father—he will testify about me."

The Holy Spirit convicts of sin and guides you into all truth.

John 16:7-13, NIV

"But very truly I tell you, it is for your good that I am going away. Unless I go away, the Advocate will not come to you; but if I go, I will send him to you. When he comes, he will prove the world to be in the wrong about sin and righteousness and judgment: about sin, because people do not believe in me; about righteousness, because I am going to the Father, where you can see me no longer; and about judgment, because the prince of this world now stands condemned.

"I have much more to say to you, more than you can now bear. But when he, the Spirit of truth, comes, he will guide you into all the truth. He will not speak on his own; he will speak only what he hears, and he will tell you what is yet to come."

The Holy Spirit's life-giving power frees you from the power of sin that leads to death.

Romans 8:2, NIV

because through Christ Jesus the law of the Spirit who gives life has set you free from the law of sin and death.

The Holy Spirit's power is available to every Christ follower. He can raise you up into new spiritual life. He can bury your old sinful nature and resurrect you by His Spirit.

Romans 8:9-11, NIV

You, however, are not in the realm of the flesh but are in the realm of the Spirit, if indeed the Spirit of God lives in you. And if anyone does not have the Spirit of Christ, they do not belong to Christ. But if Christ is in you, then even though your body is subject to death because of sin, the Spirit gives life because of righteousness. And if the Spirit of him who raised Jesus from the dead is living in you, he who raised Christ from the dead will also give life to your mortal bodies because of his Spirit who lives in you.

The Holy Spirit leads you as a son or daughter of God.

Romans 8:12-16, NIV

Therefore, brothers and sisters, we have an obligation—but it is not to the flesh, to live according to it. For if you live according to the flesh, you will die; but if by the Spirit you put to death the misdeeds of the body, you will live. For those who are led by the Spirit of God are the children of God. The Spirit you received does not make you slaves, so that you live in fear again; rather, the Spirit you received brought about your adoption to sonship. And by him we cry, *"Abba,* Father." The Spirit himself testifies with our spirit that we are God's children.

The Holy Spirit helps you in your weakness. He prays for you. No one knows you better, and no one knows the Father better than the Holy Spirit.

Romans 8:26-27, NIV

In the same way, the Spirit helps us in our weakness. We do not know what we ought to pray for, but the Spirit himself intercedes for us through wordless groans. And he who searches our hearts knows the mind of the Spirit, because the Spirit intercedes for God's people in accordance with the will of God.

The Holy Spirit knows all things. He can guide you into all truth.

1 Corinthians 2:10-16, NIV

These are the things God has revealed to us by his Spirit. The Spirit searches all things, even the deep things of God. For who knows a person's thoughts except their own spirit within them? In the same way no one knows the thoughts of God except the Spirit of God. What we have received is not the spirit of the world, but the Spirit who is from God, so that we may understand what God has freely given us. This is what we speak, not in words taught us by human wisdom but in words taught by the Spirit, explaining spiritual realities with Spirit-taught words. The person without the Spirit does not accept the things that come from the Spirit of God but considers them foolishness, and cannot understand them because they are discerned only through the Spirit. The person with the Spirit makes judgments about all things, but such a person is not subject to merely human judgments, or, "Who has known the mind of the Lord so as to instruct him?"

But we have the mind of Christ.

Your body is a temple of the Holy Spirit.

1 Corinthians 6:19-20, NIV

Do you not know that your bodies are temples of the Holy Spirit, who is in you, whom you have received from God? You are not your own; you were bought at a price. Therefore honor God with your bodies.

The Holy Spirit empowers you through spiritual gifts.

1 Corinthians 12:7-11, NIV

Now to each one the manifestation of the Spirit is given for the common good. To one there is given through the Spirit a message of wisdom, to another a message of knowledge by means of the same Spirit, to another faith by the same Spirit, to another gifts of healing by that one Spirit, to another miraculous powers, to another prophecy, to another distinguishing between spirits, to another speaking in different kinds of tongues, and to still another the interpretation of tongues. All these are the work of one and the same Spirit, and he distributes them to each one, just as he determines.

Anchor 4

The Holy Spirit can help you live out right desires so as not to be led by your sinful nature.

Galatians 5:16-21, NIV

So I say, walk by the Spirit, and you will not gratify the desires of the flesh. For the flesh desires what is contrary to the Spirit, and the Spirit what is contrary to the flesh. They are in conflict with each other, so that you are not to do whatever you want. But if you are led by the Spirit, you are not under the law. The acts of the flesh are obvious: sexual immorality, impurity and debauchery; idolatry and witchcraft; hatred, discord, jealousy, fits of rage, selfish ambition, dissensions, factions and envy; drunkenness, orgies, and the like. I warn you, as I did before, that those who live like this will not inherit the kingdom of God.

The Holy Spirit produces fruit in your life.

Galatians 5:22-23, NIV

But the fruit of the Spirit is love, joy, peace, forbearance, kindness, goodness, faithfulness, gentleness and self-control. Against such things there is no law.

The Holy Spirit keeps you until you fully experience your inheritance in Heaven.

Ephesians 1:13-14, NIV

And you also were included in Christ when you heard the message of truth, the gospel of your salvation. When you believed, you were marked in him with a seal, the promised Holy Spirit, who is a deposit guaranteeing our inheritance until the redemption of those who are God's possession—to the praise of his glory.

The Holy Spirit unites believers.

Ephesians 2:22, NIV

And in him you too are being built together to become a dwelling in which God lives by his Spirit.

The Holy Spirit can be grieved by the way you live.

Ephesians 4:30, NIV

And do not grieve the Holy Spirit of God, with whom you were sealed for the day of redemption.

The Holy Spirit inspired the very words of the Bible.

2 Peter 1:20-21, NIV

Above all, you must understand that no prophecy of Scripture came about by the prophet's own interpretation of things. For prophecy never had its origin in the human will, but prophets, though human, spoke from God as they were carried along by the Holy Spirit.

The Holy Spirit allows you to know God.

The ways of God can be mysterious. They are so far above your own ways that you could never fully understand them. However, there are many things God has intended for you to know (Deuteronomy 29:29). He has written about such things in His Word, so you may know Him better and live an abundant Christian life. The Holy Spirit is revealed to you in Scripture. As you allow Him to guide you, He continues to reveal Himself.

The story of Jesus at the well with the Samaritan woman gives a beautiful picture of how the Holy Spirit quenches our thirst once and for all (John 4:1-45). Jesus calls Himself, "Living Water." The Holy Spirit is this source of Living Water that continues to fill Christ's followers. When we drink from the well, we will never thirst again.

John 7:37-39, NIV

On the last and greatest day of the festival, Jesus stood and said in a loud voice, "Let anyone who is thirsty come to me and drink. Whoever believes in me, as Scripture has said, rivers of living water will flow from within them." By this he meant the Spirit, whom those who believed in him were later to receive. Up to that time the Spirit had not been given, since Jesus had not yet been glorified.

When He said this, Jesus had not yet died on the cross for the sins of the world. He had not been resurrected or ascended into Heaven. But He repeatedly talked about how, once He went to be with the Father, the Holy Spirit would come to be with His disciples. Later, just as Jesus promised, the Holy Spirit empowered them with the boldness, wisdom, and passion to spread the gospel in a way they never had before.

I grew up in the streets of East Harlem in New York City. One of the sayings I frequently heard growing up was, "You are full of it." What are you full of? You are either full of yourself or full of the Holy Spirit.

Think about this. Your body is the temple, the home, of the Holy Spirit. From the outside looking in, is it obvious that He lives within you? Can anyone and everyone see the presence of the Holy Spirit in your life? If so, you are filled with Him. You have allowed Him to completely fill every part of the house. You have been overtaken by a power greater than your own.

On the other hand, is the Holy Spirit put away into a corner or a closet and not given full access to His home within you? If He cannot be seen when someone looks into the "windows" of your life, then you are not filled with Him. You are limiting His power in your life and only giving Him a little space that is hidden away behind a closed door. That is a tragic scenario, if you are a Christian. It means your own power is running the show . . . and probably not all that well. The Apostle Paul reminds us in 1 Thessalonians 5:19 not to put out the Spirit's fire.

Ephesians 5:15-19, NIV

Be very careful, then, how you live—not as unwise but as wise, making the most of every opportunity, because the days are evil. Therefore do not be foolish, but understand what the Lord's will is. Do not get drunk on wine, which leads to debauchery. Instead, be filled with the Spirit, speaking to one another with psalms, hymns, and songs from the Spirit. Sing and make music from your heart to the Lord.

If you are going to be influenced by anyone, let it be the Holy Spirit. Let Him overshadow every other influence in your life. To use

Paul's words, you can be intoxicated with the power of the Holy Spirit. His influence can penetrate everything you do. You can also choose to be intoxicated with other things, but they only lead to foolishness.

God wants to influence your mind by transforming it according to His good and perfect will. Drugs and alcohol can influence thoughts and actions. The mind can regress and become easily led away from God. Paul is saying that you should not allow any influence to alter your mind or body to the point where it surpasses God's influence in your life. In other words, don't fill yourself up with other influences that can easily alter you and lead you away from God. Be wise in your choices.

You can trust the Holy Spirit to lead and guide you. The Bible gives this instruction in Galatians 5:25: "Since we are living by the Spirit, let us follow the Spirit's leading in every part of our lives." As a believer, you have the Holy Spirit. Let the Holy Spirit have you so that He will change the way you live. When you do, you will be able to say the following about Him:

1. **He is my personal Counselor.** When you yield to His counsel, He responds by rewarding you with His peace. If you reject His counsel, you forfeit His peace and blessing.

2. **He is my personal Guide.** He explains God's truth to believers. The Bible can never be fully understood unless the Person who breathed it into existence reveals and explains it to you. You would think that the disciples had the best teacher in Jesus. But, Jesus said, "The Holy Spirit will guide you into truth, and He will teach you all things" (John 16:13).

If you study Scripture like any other book or a newspaper, you will never fully understand God's Word or know how to apply it to your life. You must allow the Holy Spirit to make God's Word real to you. Have you ever read a Bible verse repeatedly for years, then suddenly it felt like it was the first time you had ever seen it? What do you think happened? The Holy Spirit made God's Word real to you. He quickened your spirit to relate to His Spirit. He illuminated your mind with wisdom and understanding

We need preachers and teachers to teach and preach God's Word—this is important—but always keep in mind the teaching in 1 John 2:27 (NIV):

> As for you the anointing that you have received from Him remains in you, and you do not need anyone to teach you. But as His anointing teaches you about all things and as that anointing is real, not counterfeit—just as it has taught you, remain in Him.

There is great danger in reading Scripture without asking the Holy Spirit to teach you and lead you into truth. As important as preachers and teachers are, you are to trust and follow the Holy Spirit above all others. As He guides you, He will make you aware of pitfalls. If you are not allowing the Holy Spirit to be your personal guide and interpreter, you open yourself up to the tricks of the devil.

The Bible is just words unless you allow the Holy Spirit to reveal its divine meaning to you. If He is not allowed to operate and lead you like this, you can fall into the habit of reading Scripture to justify what you already believe. If you are in the habit of discarding or ignoring any part of Scripture that you disagree with, you are not allowing the Holy Spirit to lead you into His truth.

In summary, knowing and understanding the Holy Spirit, allowing Him to guide your life, is absolutely necessary to a Christ follower. If you are serious about getting well, living for the Lord, and having the power to do so, you must allow the Holy Spirit to lead. You have all of Him. Does He have all of you?

PAUSE & PRAY

When Jesus was teaching His disciples how to pray, He wrapped up that teaching by saying this in Luke 11:13 (NIV):

> "If you then, though you are evil, know how to give good gifts to your children, how much more will your Father in heaven give the Holy Spirit to those who ask him!"

Prayer

Holy Spirit, I need more of You and less of me. Holy Spirit, please fill me with all of Your power, gifts, wisdom, knowledge, love, joy, peace, patience, kindness, goodness, faithfulness, gentleness, and self-control. I surrender complete control to You to fill my life with everything You have for me.

 ## Ask Yourself

Do I believe what the Bible says about the Holy Spirit?

How do I live out the Spirit-filled life?

How have I grieved the Holy Spirit? Am I currently grieving Him?

When were some moments that the Holy Spirit has given me peace, comfort, and counsel?

How is the Holy Spirit changing me from the inside out?

Write your own statement of who the Holy Spirit is to you. Share your insights from this time of reflection with your study group or a trusted individual.

⚓

ANCHOR 5

REALIZE WHO I AM IN CHRIST AND REJECT THE LIE THAT I AM MY CHARACTER DEFECTS AND SINS.

Pray

As you begin this lesson, pray that you will have an Encounter with God as you earnestly seek Him. Don't rush through reading everything and don't rush through praying. Take some time to stop and listen so you may hear what God wants to say to you. Be sure to write whatever comes to your mind in your journal as you use the following as a prayer to the Lord:

Lord, I want to hear Your voice—and Your voice alone—through Your Word and throughout this lesson.

With every scripture or compilation of scriptures, pray these specific prayers:

Lord, what are You saying in Your Word?
Lord, what are You saying to me?
Lord, how do You want me to apply this to my life?

Journal everything that comes to your mind.

Therefore, if anyone is in Christ, he is a new creation; the old has gone, the new has come!
—2 Corinthians 5:17, NIV

SEE YOURSELF THE WAY GOD SEES YOU

In Anchor 3, we learned that our old life and sins are crucified when we place our trust in Jesus Christ. Living out that faith by allowing our new life in Christ to replace our old habits, requires commitment, discipline, and obedience.

According to 2 Corinthians 5:17, a real transaction took place when you trusted Jesus as your Savior. You were made new! You were forgiven. You were given a new nature. A new identity. In other words, you are now a different person. You may not feel different, but you are different. You may not feel forgiven, but you are forgiven. You are born again and are no longer defined by what you do, what you did, or what has been done to you. You are now defined by what God calls you. Period.

God's desire is for you to walk in that new identity and see yourself as He does. God wants you to be accepted, secure, and know your significance in Christ. This is one of the benefits you inherited through Jesus's work on the cross.

Your life should be a reflection of what Christ did for you. If you are to follow His commands, it can only be done through His power and in the new identity He has given you. God does not want you to spend the rest of your life trying to discover who you already are. If you don't know who you are, your purpose or direction will be shaky. But if you live in your true identity in Christ, your direction in life becomes crystal clear.

PUTTING ON YOUR NEW IDENTITY

Romans 6:6, NLT

We know that our old sinful selves were crucified with Christ so that sin might lose its power in our lives. We are no longer slaves to sin.

Colossians 3:7-10, NIV

You used to walk in these ways, in the life you once lived. But now you must also rid yourselves of all such things as these: anger, rage, malice, slander, and filthy language from your lips. Do not lie to each other, since you have taken off your old self with its practices and have put on the new self, which is being renewed in knowledge in the image of its Creator.

Ephesians 4:22-24, NIV

You were taught, with regard to your former way of life, to put off your old self, which is being corrupted by its deceitful desires; to be made new in the attitude of your minds; and to put on the new self, created to be like God in true righteousness and holiness.

There was a decisive and definitive *past* action that occurred the moment you received the gift of salvation through Jesus Christ (Romans 6:6, Colossians 3:7-10). But, as one who has been born again, you are to apply a *continuous* action—take off your old self and put on the new (Ephesians 4:22-24). This daily action requires intentionality.

Think of it in this manner. Before you knew Jesus as your Lord and Savior, you wore the filthy stained garments of sin. But, when you received Jesus Christ into your life, His righteousness washed away those filthy garments of sin. Once you have been washed clean, why would you want to put those filthy garments back on?

The death of Jesus on the cross paid for the salvation of all who believe and follow Him. Paul is not telling us to do for ourselves what

Christ has already done. Instead, Paul is saying that you are a new creation in Christ and must become what God has already declared you to be. You must have the resolve to resist your way of life to walk in the new life God has given.

Galatians 3:27, NIV

for all of you who were baptized into Christ have clothed your-selves with Christ.

Romans 13:14, NIV

Rather, clothe yourselves with the Lord Jesus Christ, and do not think about how to gratify the desires of the flesh.

The phrase "clothe yourselves" is also translated as "put on" in the above verses; specifically, "putting on" the life of Christ. To clothe oneself with a person, or to "put on" a person, is to take on the characteristics of that person and become like them.

As believers, you are not trying to become children of God. You already *are* a child of God who's in the process of becoming more like Jesus. As you continue to affirm who you are in Christ, your behavior will begin to reflect it. You will know who you are, what your purpose is, and where you are going.

IDENTITY STORY

Early in Scripture, there is an account of Jacob wrestling with God (Genesis 32). Jacob's very name, in fact, means "he grasps the heel." He was a twin who was born after his brother, Esau. The implication is that he could have been trying to grab Esau's heel to get ahead of him at birth. Apparently, he had been wrestling from the beginning.

Later in life, Jacob tricked his father, Isaac, and stole Esau's birthright as the firstborn son. After Esau threatened to kill Jacob, he went on the run for twenty years. But Jacob was now about to come face-to-face with Esau again. He was afraid of what would happen. Jacob prayed that God would save him from his brother. He reminded God of the promises He had made to him.

That night on the bank of the Jordan River, Jacob wrestled with a man all night long. Jacob wouldn't give in. The man told Jacob to let him go because it was daybreak. Jacob must have finally realized who he was wrestling with because he saw the face of God in the daylight and said, "I will not let you go unless you bless me." Jacob used his persistence to acquire a blessing, and God gave him a new name. An encounter with God will change you forever.

He asked Jacob, "What is your name?" When Jacob told Him, He said, "Your name will no longer be Jacob, but Israel, because you have struggled with God and with men and have overcome." He gave Jacob the blessing he requested.

Throughout the Bible, God gave people new names to mark the changes He made in their lives and to give them a new direction for the future. Jacob had come a long way from the younger man who tricked his father and stole his brother's birthright. His persistence had once been used for selfish gain, but God had changed him. Jacob's persistence had become something that he used to fulfill the promises of God to his nation, Israel.

 Can you identify with this story? Think about your life. Reflect on times when you have been selfish. Think about the changes God has made or is making in your life.

Consider your life before you came to know God. Do you think He wants you to be that same person and to do those same things?

Just like Jacob, God calls you someone else now. He wants to continually transform you to live for His purposes. God calls you to be someone other than who you used to be, someone new, with new and right desires. Someone who has a past but is no longer identified by it. You are made in the image of God, and He delights in making you into what He intends for you to become—His masterpiece.

You may not realize this, but there's a spiritual war going on over your identity. Satan spends most of his time taking what God has created for good and trying to destroy it. He knows if he can keep you from being *you* by creating an identity crisis, it will lead to chaos and eventually destroy your life. How does Satan keep you from knowing your true identity?

Many times, Satan uses pain in your life to deceive and disguise your true identity. If he can get you to be resentful or overwhelmed with guilt, shame, and regret, you will forget that you are a child of God. This is a huge issue. Unresolved pain creates character defects. A lot of people think that, because they have certain sinful tendencies (e.g., lusts, faults, habits, etc.), it is who they are. They identify themselves with a particular behavior, thought pattern, or desire.

Some say that the first step to facing our problem is admitting that we have one. While there may be some measure of truth to this, don't be fooled into thinking you *are* your problem. For example, "My name is Joe, and I am an alcoholic" may sound like you are admitting that you have a problem, but it is also self-defeating. The misconception is that you are your sins—that your bad habits are your identity.

But you *are not* your defects. You *are not* your faults. You *are not* your sins. They may be something you have done, but they are not your identity. They are not who you are. It helps to look at God's Word and the life of Jesus to know the truth. His life could easily be summarized by these three statements:

1. He knew who He was.

2. He knew His purpose.

3. He knew where He was going.

If you take a close look at His life, you will find that His identity was under attack from the moment He was baptized until His death on the cross (Luke 23:35). He had to deal with a barrage of insults, lies, temptations, and challenging voices (Matthew 4:3-6). Satan knew that if he could get the Son of God to doubt His identity, he would stop the purpose of Jesus. But the Son of God came to destroy the works of the devil (1 John 3:8). Ultimately, Satan could not stop God's plan. He was destined for defeat, but it didn't stop him from trying.

The Bible says that Jesus was tempted in every way but never once sinned. He knew who He was. He knew His purpose. And He knew where He was going. If Jesus was tempted and challenged in His identity to the maximum degree, then we can expect to be tempted and challenged in the same way. Like Christ, we need to be ready with the truth of God and His Word.

LIVING IN VICTORY

Defeated Christians typically have two things in common: They don't know who they are in Christ, and they don't understand what it means to be a child of God. The enemy wants to keep you from knowing your true identity because if you really believed what God says about you, **you might just start living that way!**

Consider the following changes that could happen when believers walk in the ways of Jesus:

- If you really believed you were forgiven, you wouldn't walk around with constant guilt and shame. (Romans 8:1)

- If you really believed that you are accepted by God, you wouldn't look for your acceptance from other people.

- If you really believed you are secure, you wouldn't be so consumed with the things of this world.

- If you really believed you are significant in Christ, you would live your life with confidence and not succumb to codependent behaviors.

- If you really believed you have the mind of Christ, you would start taking your thoughts captive to the obedience of Christ and be better equipped to resist temptations. (1 Corinthians 2:16)

- If you really believed that God lives in you, you wouldn't feel so alone and would let Him guide your life.

- If you really believed that God calls you holy, redeemed, sanctified, perfect, justified, friend, highly loved, highly favored, chosen, a royal priesthood, complete, free from condemnation, the object of His affection, a saint, a child ... if you really believed that, you would start living that way. (1 Peter 2:9-10)

Satan continues to tell you that you are a sinner. God calls believers "saints" and declares them righteous not because they are good or sinless but because of what Jesus has done for them. A believer is a saint who still sins, but one who sins less and less. In other words, sinning is something you may still do, but it is not who you are.

When you see the words "sinners" and "saints" in the Bible, they are identity statements. A sinner refers to someone who is not a follower of Jesus. Followers of Jesus are called saints. Those are identities, not behaviors. We are not sinners saved by grace. We *were* sinners that were saved by grace. We are *now* saints that still sin and who still need grace.

Satan may try to convince you that your identity comes from what you do. God says that your identity comes from what He has already done for you. You are the person He calls you, not who the world calls you or even who you call yourself. Tragically, many Christians will spend an entire lifetime trying to become someone they already are. If you are a follower of Jesus, God doesn't say you have to wait to become who He made you to be. He declares that this is your identity now.

Perhaps the biggest obstacle to knowing our true identity in Christ is the fact that we look for acceptance, security, and significance in all the wrong places. These three basic psychological needs are felt by everyone. And we have sought fulfillment in many places outside of a personal relationship with Jesus Christ. When we look for those three things in other people, in this world, and through ourselves and our accomplishments, we end up in an identity crisis.

There are approximately 140 scriptures in the New Testament that validate our *acceptance, security,* and *significance* in Christ. The following are only a handful:

ACCEPTANCE

Realizing that you are accepted by God in Christ is where your identity starts.

I am God's child.

John 1:12, NIV

Yet to all who did receive him, to those who believed in his name, he gave the right to become children of God—

I am Jesus Christ's friend.

John 15:15, NIV

"I no longer call you servants, because a servant does not know his master's business. Instead, I have called you friends, for everything that I learned from my Father I have made known to you."

I have been justified before God by Christ.

Romans 5:1, NIV

Therefore, since we have been justified through faith, we have peace with God through our Lord Jesus Christ,

I have been bought with a price. I belong to God.

1 Corinthians 6:20, NIV

you were bought at a price. Therefore honor God with your bodies.

I am a saint.

Ephesians 1:1, BSB

To the saints in Ephesus, the faithful in Christ Jesus:

I am holy and blameless in His sight.

Ephesians 1:4, NIV

For he chose us in him before the creation of the world to be holy and blameless in his sight

I have direct access to God through the Holy Spirit.

Ephesians 2:18, NIV

For through him we both have access to the Father by one Spirit.

I have been redeemed and forgiven of all my sins.

Colossians 1:14, ESV

in whom we have redemption, the forgiveness of sins.

I am complete in Christ.

Colossians 2:10, NKJV

and you are complete in Him

SECURITY

Ultimate security is not found in your career, marriage, ministry, or any other person. Your security is found in Christ alone.

I am free forever from condemnation.

Romans 8:1, NIV

Therefore, there is now no condemnation for those who are in Christ Jesus,

I am free from any condemning charges against me.

Romans 8:33, NIV

Who will bring any charge against those whom God has chosen? It is God who justifies.

I cannot be separated from the love of God.

Romans 8:39, NIV

neither height nor depth, nor anything else in all creation, will be able to separate us from the love of God that is in Christ Jesus our Lord.

I stand firm in Christ and have been established, anointed, and sealed by God.

2 Corinthians 1:21-22, NIV

Now it is God who makes both us and you stand firm in Christ. He anointed us, set his seal of ownership on us, and put his Spirit in our hearts as a deposit, guaranteeing what is to come.

I am hidden with Christ in God.

Colossians 3:3, NIV

For you died, and your life is now hidden with Christ in God.

I am a citizen of Heaven.

Philippians 3:20, NIV

But our citizenship is in heaven.

SIGNIFICANCE

We all want our lives to count for something. God knew this and designed us to have significance in all things.

I am the salt and light of the earth.

Matthew 5:13-14, NIV

"You are the salt of the earth. But if the salt loses its saltiness, how can it be made salty again? It is no longer good for anything, except to be thrown out and trampled underfoot. You are the light of the world. A town built on a hill cannot be hidden."

I am a branch of the true vine and a channel of His life.
John 15:5, NIV

"I am the vine; you are the branches. If you remain in me and I in you, you will bear much fruit; apart from me you can do nothing."

I have been chosen and appointed to bear fruit that will last.

John 15:16, NIV

"You did not choose me, but I chose you and appointed you so that you might go and bear fruit—fruit that will last—and so that whatever you ask in my name the Father will give you."

I am a personal witness of Jesus Christ.

Acts 1:8, NIV

"But you will receive power when the Holy Spirit comes on you; and you will be my witnesses in Jerusalem, and in all Judea and Samaria, and to the ends of the earth."

I am God's temple.

1 Corinthians 3:16, NIV

Don't you know that you yourselves are God's temple and that God's Spirit dwells in your midst?

I am a minister of reconciliation for God.

2 Corinthians 5:19, NIV

that God was reconciling the world to himself in Christ, not counting people's sins against them. And he has committed to us the message of reconciliation.

I am God's coworker.

2 Corinthians 6:1, NIV

As God's coworkers we urge you not to receive God's grace in vain.

Anchor 5

I am an ambassador for Christ.

2 Corinthians 5:20, NIV

We are therefore Christ's ambassadors, as though God were making his appeal through us.

I am part of a chosen people, a royal priesthood, a holy nation, a people belonging to God.

1 Peter 2:9, NIV

But you are a chosen people, a royal priesthood, a holy nation, God's special possession, that you may declare the praises of him who called you out of darkness into his wonderful light.

I am seated with Jesus in the heavenly realms.

Ephesians 2:6, NIV

And God raised us up with Christ and seated us with him in the heavenly realms in Christ Jesus

I am God's workmanship.

Ephesians 2:10, NKJV

For we are His workmanship, created in Christ Jesus for good works, which God prepared beforehand that we should walk in them.

I may approach God with freedom and confidence.

Ephesians 3:12, NIV

In him and through faith in him we may approach God with freedom and confidence.

WHAT'S NEXT?

Journal an identity statement about yourself based on the scriptures we just covered. Include statements of acceptance, security, and significance in Christ.

Bill's Identity Statement

This is my identity statement from my journaling of this lesson. I titled it, "I am who the great I AM says I am!"

My name is child of the one true King. I am forgiven. I am redeemed. I am accepted. I am secure. I am significant. I am a promise keeper recipient of the only true promise keeper. I am a citizen of Heaven and not of this world. I am a kingdom representative on a Kingdom assignment based on who I am in Christ for the time I have in this world. I am a free person set free from the bondage of sin, shame, lies, my past, my guilt, my regrets, my doubts, fears, insecurities, character defects, lies and tactics of the enemy, and anything or anyone else that opposes the truth of who I am in Christ.

I am a new creation in Christ. The old is gone, dead, and buried. I have been raised from the dead spiritually because I am a born-again follower of Jesus Christ.

I am a Spirit-filled, Spirit-minded, Spirit-guided temple of the Holy Spirit. I am seated with God. I am an heir to the throne. I am an ambassador of reconciliation. I am a royal priesthood who is the priest of my home and a called priest unto my God operating under the anointing and calling of the Holy Spirit. In Christ, I am a personally handcrafted masterpiece by God for His pleasure to be used for His purposes.

In Christ, I am secure in my calling, in my destiny, in my destination, in my trials, in my failures, and in my victories. I am victorious in Christ and no longer a victim but a victor. In Christ, I am a blood-bought, blood-washed, blood-sanctified, blood-marked soldier for the King, and no weapon formed against me will ever prosper. In Christ, I can do all things through Christ who gives me strength. In Christ, I am an overcomer who will go through trouble but will take heart because Jesus has overcome the world. In Christ, I am who God says I am because the great I AM said I am and that settles the issue.

No one can argue with me on these facts. No one can dispute them. They are indisputable. No one can change my mind because I now have the mind of Christ and to call me a liar would in essence be saying that God is a liar.

In Christ, I am not the Great I AM, but I am all these things in Christ because my daddy in Heaven said I am!

Read 1 John 3:1 (NIV) aloud, with conviction:

See what great love the Father has lavished on us, that we should be called children of God. And that is what we are!

The next time you introduce yourself to someone, instead of leading with the sin that so easily entangles you, lead with the truth of who you are by saying, "Hi. My name is _____. I am the one who Jesus loves. I am a child of the King!"

 ## Ask Yourself

What are some of my patterns of thinking and acting as my "old self"?

What are some of my patterns of thinking and acting in my "new nature"?

How have I looked for acceptance, security, and significance outside of a relationship with Jesus Christ?

How have events, people, and society shaped and distorted my identity?

Share with your discussion group or a trusted individual the identity statement you wrote about yourself based on the scriptures you studied.

⚓

ANCHOR 6

GET HONEST ABOUT MY PAST AND LET THE HOLY SPIRIT REVEAL AND RIP OUT THE ROOT ISSUES OF MY LIFE.

Pray

As you begin this lesson, pray that you will have an Encounter with God as you earnestly seek Him. Don't rush through reading everything and don't rush through praying. Take some time to stop and listen so you may hear what God wants to say to you. Be sure to write whatever comes to your mind in your journal as you use the following as a prayer to the Lord:

Lord, I want to hear Your voice—and Your voice alone— through Your Word and throughout this lesson.

With every scripture or compilation of scriptures, pray these specific prayers:

Lord, what are You saying in Your Word?
Lord, what are You saying to me?
Lord, how do You want me to apply this to my life?

Journal everything that comes to your mind.

Yes, what joy for those whose record the Lord has cleared of guilt, whose lives are lived in complete honesty!
—Psalm 32:2, NLT

IT'S TIME TO GET HONEST

Once you apply them to your life, the first five Anchors of Hope will put you in a great position to heal and grow. By making the decision to get well and realizing that you do a terrible job at trying to be God, you allow His loving power to restore hope and healing in your life. By surrendering your life to Jesus Christ, you are no longer the same person. The finished work of Christ on the cross has given you a new identity in Christ. God has declared you "not guilty." You are forgiven, once and for all time; you now have an eternal home in Heaven. And while you are still living in this world, the Holy Spirit enables you to know and walk in your new identity in Christ.

But now, before healing can continue, you have to get honest with God, yourself, and others about your past. Getting honest with yourself and others is part of the healing process. It means you understand that He knows everything about you already, yet still loves you, but you are choosing to get brutally honest about anything you have not spoken to Him about up to this point.

If you allow Him to do so, God can remove the residue from the past that might hinder your freedom in the future. But it will take an honest evaluation. When you evaluate your past, God can reveal root issues that have influenced your behavior over the years. People, events, coping mechanisms, fears, insecurities, doubt, pain, and habits swirl together in forming the person you are today.

The sixth Anchor of Hope requires getting gut-level honest so that you can identify patterns of the past and allow God to reveal and heal the root issues. Anchor 6 will call you to:

1. **Have the right mindset** by agreeing with God on the thoughts He wants you to dwell on and the truths He wants you to live out.

2. **Have the right attitude** by humbly allowing God to evaluate your thoughts and guide your actions through His Word.

3. **Have the right motive by loving God from a place of gratitude**. In the past, you may have seen God as a convenient bailout whenever life got difficult. Now that you have a real relationship with God, you can be motivated from a place of love.

4. **Have the right spirit of complete honesty** by allowing the Holy Spirit to search your heart so you do not get stuck in the events or habits of the past.

PAUSE & PRAY

Begin putting these four things into practice by meditating on the following scriptures and asking God to reveal His truths in your life:

Ask God to give you the same heart and passion for His truth.

Psalm 119:9-18, NIV

How can a young person stay on the path of purity?
  By living according to your word.
I seek you with all my heart;
  do not let me stray from your commands.
I have hidden your word in my heart
  that I might not sin against you.
Praise be to you, Lord;
  teach me your decrees.
With my lips I recount
  all the laws that come from your mouth.
I rejoice in following your statutes
  as one rejoices in great riches.

I meditate on your precepts
　and consider your ways.
I delight in your decrees;
　I will not neglect your word.
Be good to your servant while I live,
　that I may obey your word.
Open my eyes that I may see
　wonderful things in your law.

Psalm 119:67-68, NIV

Before I was afflicted I went astray,
　but now I obey your word.
You are good, and what you do is good;
　teach me your decrees.

Psalm 119:73-74, NIV

Your hands made me and formed me;
　give me understanding to learn your commands.
May those who fear you rejoice when they see me,
　for I have put my hope in your word.

Psalm 119: 105-106, NIV

Your word is a lamp for my feet,
　a light on my path.
I have taken an oath and confirmed it,
　that I will follow your righteous laws.

Ask God for the same type of godly sorrow and repentance.

Psalm 51:1-12, NIV

Have mercy on me, O God,
　according to your unfailing love;
according to your great compassion
　blot out my transgressions.
Wash away all my iniquity
　and cleanse me from my sin.

For I know my transgressions,
   and my sin is always before me.
Against you, you only, have I sinned
   and done what is evil in your sight;
so you are right in your verdict
   and justified when you judge.
Surely I was sinful at birth,
   sinful from the time my mother conceived me.
Yet you desired faithfulness even in the womb;
   you taught me wisdom in that secret place.

Cleanse me with hyssop, and I will be clean;
   wash me, and I will be whiter than snow.
Let me hear joy and gladness;
   let the bones you have crushed rejoice.
Hide your face from my sins
   and blot out all my iniquity.

Create in me a pure heart, O God,
   and renew a steadfast spirit within me.
Do not cast me from your presence
   or take your Holy Spirit from me.
Restore to me the joy of your salvation
   and grant me a willing spirit, to sustain me.

Ask God to remind you of just how much you have been forgiven by Him.

Psalm 130:3-4, NIV

If you, Lord, kept a record of sins,
   Lord, who could stand?
But with you there is forgiveness,
   so that we can, with reverence, serve you.

Ask God to help you get honest about your past.

Isaiah 43:25-26, NIV

"I, even I, am he who blots out
  your transgressions, for my own sake,
  and remembers your sins no more.
Review the past for me,
  let us argue the matter together;
  state the case for your innocence."

Ask God to give you the desire to have that same kind of honesty with yourself, with others, and with Him.

1 John 1:5-10, NIV

This is the message we have heard from him and declare to you: God is light; in him there is no darkness at all. If we claim to have fellowship with him and yet walk in the darkness, we lie and do not live out the truth. But if we walk in the light, as he is in the light, we have fellowship with one another, and the blood of Jesus, his Son, purifies us from all sin.

If we claim to be without sin, we deceive ourselves and the truth is not in us. If we confess our sins, he is faithful and just and will forgive us our sins and purify us from all unrighteousness. If we claim we have not sinned, we make him out to be a liar and his word is not in us.

Ask God to help you be honest about any sin in your life that slows you down and trips you up so you may be able to run the race well and keep your eyes on Jesus.

Hebrews 12:1-2, NIV

Therefore, since we are surrounded by such a great cloud of witnesses, let us throw off everything that hinders and the sin that so easily entangles. And let us run with perseverance the race marked out for us, fixing our eyes on Jesus, the pioneer and perfecter of faith. For the joy set before him he endured the cross, scorning its shame, and sat down at the right hand of the throne of God.

Ask God to search every part of you through His Word and Holy Spirit.

Hebrews 4:12-13, NIV

For the word of God is alive and active. Sharper than any double-edged sword, it penetrates even to dividing soul and spirit, joints and marrow; it judges the thoughts and attitudes of the heart. Nothing in all creation is hidden from God's sight. Everything is uncovered and laid bare before the eyes of him to whom we must give account.

Anchor 6 can be scary for some people. It may even be scary for you. It is this anchor, however, that separates those who only talk about getting well from those who actually do. Applying Anchor 6 to your life allows God to get to the root issues of anything that keeps you stuck and heal those areas in your life. In the process, God shows you a better way to respond to what people and events have done to you in the past so you can move forward in the future.

GOD WILL MAKE OUR PAST OUR *PAST*

Read Psalm 32 and meditate on its truths. As you do, ask God for the same sort of humility and brokenness you see in the passage.

Psalm 32, NLT

Oh, what joy for those whose disobedience is forgiven, whose sin is put out of sight! Yes, what joy for those whose record the LORD has cleared of guilt, whose lives are lived in complete honesty! When I refused to confess my sin, my body wasted away, and I groaned all day long. Day and night your hand of discipline was heavy on me. My strength evaporated like water in the summer heat. *Interlude*

Finally, I confessed all my sins to you and stopped trying to hide my guilt. I said to myself, "I will confess my rebellion to the LORD." And you forgave me! All my guilt is gone.   *Interlude*

Therefore, let all the godly pray to you while there is still time, that they may not drown in the floodwaters of judgment. For you are my hiding place; you protect me from trouble. You surround me with songs of victory.   *Interlude*

The LORD says, "I will guide you along the best pathway for your life. I will advise you and watch over you. Do not be like a senseless horse or mule that needs a bit and bridle to keep it under control." Many sorrows come to the wicked, but unfailing love surrounds those who trust the LORD. So rejoice in the Lord and be glad, all you who obey him! Shout for joy, all you whose hearts are pure!

David called upon God for deliverance. He recognized that God could do what he could not. When he confessed his sins to the Lord and repented of them, David encountered the joy of forgiveness. His guilt was taken away. God will do that for anyone who calls upon Him; that includes you!

Toward the end of the psalm, we learn that God will instruct you in the way that you should go. He will counsel you and watch over you. In other words, you can do things God's way, or you can do things your own way. Your way, however, will only cause pain, whereas God's ways will surround you with His unfailing love. He gently instructs you to have a pure heart and to rejoice in the Lord.

In the historical Lincoln-Douglas debates in 1858, Abraham Lincoln said, "You can fool all the people some of the time and some of the people all the time, but you cannot fool all the people all the time." How true that statement is. You may have some people fooled into believing that all is well, but others can see glimpses of issues or dysfunction in your life. In fact, you may have even fooled yourself into believing that circumstances or relationships in your life are all okay. You lie to yourself repeatedly by pretending that you are fine, but you are not fine at all. More importantly, God is never fooled by you or by anyone. He already knows every detail of your life. And He isn't shocked when you come to Him and get honest about your "stuff." He is loving and forgiving and offers to put the righteousness of Christ onto you. It hardly seems fair, nevertheless, it is the way of our Heavenly Father.

PAUSE & PRAY

Read Psalm 139:1-18 and Psalm 139:23-24 as a prayer of humility and honesty to God. Ask God to remind you of His great love. Invite Him to do these four things:

1. *Search me and know my heart.*

2. *Test me and know my anxious thoughts.*

3. *Point out anything in me that offends You.*

4. *Lead me along Your path.*

After you allow God to search, test, point, and lead you, *then* God will begin to heal. He can take every ounce of pain, shame, guilt, and fear that you have experienced and help you discover who you truly are: His redeemed masterpiece.

While it is true that you cannot change or fix the past, you can be free from it. It doesn't have to hold you hostage. You have no control over the things that have already happened to you, but you do have control over how you respond to them. With God's help, you can choose healthier responses.

The Holy Spirit has a divine way of bringing light into every crevice of your life. He can expose that which has lurked in the darkness and held you captive for so long. God can help you to see things for what they really are and reveal to you the havoc they may have caused. When these things are brought to light, God can begin to heal the pain they have caused.

We are all unique, and so are our pasts. For reasons that can't always be explained or understood, some people seem to have more painful lives than others. Yet allowing God to search your heart to reveal the good, the bad, and the ugly can still greatly benefit your spiritual and relational growth. Looking back and taking an honest assessment of your life doesn't mean you are looking at just the bad stuff. If you focus only on the negatives, you will become discouraged, Some may try to skip over certain areas of their life simply because of how painful it is. If this starts to happen, take a time out and try to focus on something good from your past. Maybe your past was 99 percent bad, but focus on the 1 percent that was good. Being grateful for the good will encourage you. Allow God to give you a balanced view of both the good and the bad. Seek His comfort and truth as He leads you to freedom.

We can complicate the evaluation of our lives and make it more burdensome than it has to be. God doesn't keep a record of your forgiven sins, nor does He want you walking around with guilt and shame over something for which He has already forgiven you.

Once you have allowed God to do a thorough examination and you have confessed and turned away from your past and present sins, God forgives you of them. There is no need to revisit old sins. Guilt and shame from the enemy is used to lead you away from the cross and away from God's grace. Satan loves to condemn you. Conviction from God is just the opposite. It is meant for your good. You can turn from your sins and turn toward the God who brings hope and joy.

GOD'S GREAT EXCHANGE PROGRAM

God wants you to have healthy relationships. If you are allowing your past or present dysfunctional relationships and unresolved hurts to affect you or dictate your behavior, your relationship with God can become skewed.

God does not want you living with unresolved hurts from your past. God wants to break *all* your chains so you can live free and allow nothing to get in the way of a loving relationship between you and Him and others.

Whether or not it was your fault, God wants to heal you of all the damage that has been done. He wants to restore what the enemy has stolen. He wants to replace your regrets with hope for the future. Through His great exchange program, God does so much for you:

- He exchanges your life with His.

- He exchanges your shame with His Son.

- He exchanges your guilt with His grace.

- He exchanges your sin with His forgiveness.

- He exchanges your hate with His love.

- He exchanges your pain with His power.

- He exchanges your hurts with His healing.

- He exchanges your bad habits and character defects with His Holy Spirit.

- He exchanges your identity with His identity.

- He exchanges your old nature with His new nature.

- He exchanges your hopelessness with His eternal hope.

BILL'S PERSONAL STORY

I gave my life to Christ when I was thirty-seven years old, but I had the social skills of an immature teenager. I hadn't grown emotionally or socially beyond the hurt of the sexual assault that I experienced when I was twelve years old. My confusion and pain grew into shame and that shame grew into anger. To cope with the anger, I began drinking excessively and using drugs. In an attempt to numb my pain, I started having inappropriate sexual relationships with women when I was a very young teenager.

I never had a father, but when I became old enough to see that other people had fathers, I wondered why my own hadn't loved me enough to stick around and be my dad. The sexual assault I experienced as a child only added to my hurt and confusion. I was angry. I acted out in ways that were hurtful to me and to others. I didn't realize I had deep abandonment issues until later in life. I became a train wreck and my life was a real mess!

When I eventually received Jesus and followed Him as my Lord and Savior, I knew God needed to change me and transform my way of thinking and acting. By applying the principles of Anchor 6 to my life, I was able to connect the dots and see where people and events in my life had contributed to the person I had become. As I prayed and allowed the Holy Spirit to search my heart and reveal things to me, I started writing:

1. *Who* had done things to me

2. *What* they had done to me

3. *How* those people or those events made me feel

4. *How* I responded to the feelings those people or events created in me

5. *How* I coped with my feelings and pain towards those people or events

6. *What* character defects and/or bad habits had developed in my life, and what behaviors I exhibited as a result of what people did to me or how an event in my life impacted me

Then, I could clearly see how I had become the person I was and had done the things I had done for so many years.

Doing this spiritual exercise helped me understand the root issues in my life that had impacted me the most and shaped the person I had become. I began to understand God's will for me, and I realized that He offered a better way of life. God wanted to give me a hope and a future so I could discover my true and right identity.

Did I want to look back at my past or relive those painful memories again? Of course not! But I knew that God was with me and would not allow me to go through it alone. I knew that, for me to gain God's healing, I had to allow Him to help me revisit that stuff one more time. I had to allow God to heal me at the root issues of my life and accept His grace, truth, and love.

I discovered the things that happened to me in my past had created a path of destruction, pain, and guilt in my life. Before I believed in Jesus and decided to follow Him, I gave those hurts unhealthy power in my life. I lived as if they belonged there. I developed habits that continually allowed them to influence my bad behaviors. When I decided to follow Jesus, I didn't want to live in those hurts any more. I was ready for God's healing and deliverance.

Like a cancer, my unresolved hurts had eaten away at me for years. I believed the lie that my pain would go away over time and that it would all get better. I denied that the people and the events in my life had any effect on me. I had tried to play God by moving forward in my own way, but I was woefully unsuccessful. Unfortunately, I learned the hard way that no one is qualified to deal with guilt except Jesus Christ. I was not qualified to be God or do God's job. I had lived like this for thirty-six years. I finally decided that I wanted to get well.

Something God revealed to me, as I sought Him and His truth, was that I had majored in the minors most of my life. The symptoms of my pain were my minors—excessive use of drugs, alcohol, and sex. I had allowed those symptoms to dominate my life. But they were not the root issues of my pain. The abandonment of a father, the trauma of sexual assault, and the disappointment of losing my dreams had caused me to use those things to numb myself in unhealthy ways.

When I finally got serious about my relationship with Jesus Christ, I allowed the Holy Spirit to show me the root issues in my life. When God brought them to the surface, He illuminated what was once darkness and brought it into His marvelous light. He began to deliver me from the pain of my past. It no longer had power over me.

The enemy's lies held me hostage for most of my life. He had convinced me that I was not worthy of God's love and that I should live in guilt, shame, and regret. My own dad had not loved me enough to stay. The devil taunted me that I was unlovable and that there must be something wrong with me. But God exposed those lies and declared me not guilty. God convinced me that His plan for me was so much better than all the lies the devil had led me to believe.

Jesus said, "The thief comes only to steal and kill and destroy; I have come that they may have life, and have it to the full" (John 10:10, NIV). God opened my eyes to see and gave me wisdom to understand how the enemy had tried to derail my life. I had ridden on that train of lies as a hostage to my pain for far too long.

This personal story began with a fact that my earthly father abandoned me. It ends with a truth that my Heavenly Father never left me. The finished work of Jesus Christ on the cross declares me a son of the one true King. His arms were open wide to forgive me and to receive me when I turned from my sins and turned to Him. His grace surrounds me. His love overwhelms me. My story has become *His* story. My past is my past. My future is in Christ. I will forever live my life in gratitude and praise to the God who saved me from myself.

ALLOW GOD TO MAKE HIS STORY YOUR STORY

Take some time to be alone with God. Pray for His guidance as you seek Him. It is wise to schedule this time with God so you won't be rushed and God is given all the time He needs to do whatever He needs to do in you. Examining and evaluating your life is not a quick endeavor. You didn't get where you are overnight. However, with the counsel and comfort of the Holy Spirit, you can have revelation and healing. God can do a work in you to the degree that you are willing to be open, honest, and surrendered to Him. If you are up for the healing, He is the ultimate Healer. Take that step toward Him. He will meet you where you are and do the work required to heal you and set you free.

Answering the following questions will help you in your evaluation of your life. You will share your answers in your Encounter Study group. If you need more time or want to share your answers in more depth, feel free to schedule some time this week with an accountability partner or a trusted friend. This is not required, but it can be helpful in your process of sharing and healing.

Ask Yourself

What people and events from my past have hurt me? How did those hurts make me feel?

How did I respond and cope?

Have I hurt others in my life? How did I hurt them?

How has shame and guilt continued to hold me hostage to my past?

What regrets do I still carry?

What character defects, insecurities, fears, identity issues, or bad habits were developed in my life as a result of things that happened in my past? What character defects do I still struggle with?

What are the root issues of my life that God has revealed to me?

Please don't miss the purpose of answering these questions and doing this exercise honestly and completely. It is for your ultimate benefit and your spiritual and relational growth. There is healing in revealing what has been kept in secret. The Bible says to confess your sins to one another *so that* you may be healed (James 5:16). Healing can also occur as you talk openly about what has caused pain in your life, regardless of who was at fault. Exposing that hurt diminishes the power it has to hold you hostage to your past. As you surrender it to God, He can heal you and set you free from your past. That healing will further develop your character and help you discover God's best for your life.

⚓ ANCHOR 7

EMBRACE DISCIPLESHIP AS THE PATHWAY TO TRANSFORMATION.

Pray

As you begin this lesson, pray that you will have an Encounter with God as you earnestly seek Him. Don't rush through reading everything and don't rush through praying. Take some time to stop and listen so you may hear what God wants to say to you. Be sure to write whatever comes to your mind in your journal as you use the following as a prayer to the Lord:

Lord, I want to hear Your voice—and Your voice alone—through Your Word and throughout this lesson.

With every scripture or compilation of scriptures, pray these specific prayers:

Lord, what are You saying in Your Word?
Lord, what are You saying to me?
Lord, how do You want me to apply this to my life?

Journal everything that comes to your mind.

Therefore, I urge you, brothers and sisters, in view of God's mercy, to offer your bodies as a living sacrifice, holy and pleasing to God—this is your true and proper worship. Do not conform to the pattern of this world, but be transformed by the renewing of your mind. Then you will be able to test and approve what God's will is—his good, pleasing and perfect will.

—Romans 12:1-2, NIV

BE TRANSFORMED

Central to Christianity, Romans 12:1-2 gives clear direction to followers of Jesus on how to respond to all God has done. Within it, we find the key to personal transformation in our lives as Christ followers.

Some have equated the verse to the children's song-and-dance, "The Hokey Pokey." You start by putting a foot, then an arm, then a leg into a circle and shaking them before you "turn yourself around."

Just in case you've never heard of "The Hokey Pokey," there's one more part at the end. You have to "put your whole self in." And like the song says, that's what it's all about.

Consider how much of yourself you are willing to *put in* to be *turned around*, to be transformed. We never truly worship God fully until we put our whole selves into following Him. This translates into offering your body as a living and holy sacrifice to Him. To play on words, it requires going in *wholly* to become *holy*. Real worship happens when you confess your sin to God, turn from it, and offer yourself wholeheartedly to Him.

In his prior writings, Paul demonstrated God's mercy and goodness. Here, he reaches this conclusion: ***In view of God's mercy* (1 John 1:9)** and ***because of all He has done*** for them, ***believers should respond in true worship by giving their bodies as a living sacrifice to God.***

92

To follow this command requires that you first consider all God has done for you. It means that you must stop and recognize His mercy. You must think of how sin imprisoned you to a death sentence with no hope of parole. His life was sacrificed as the only acceptable substitute for your sins. That is a big price. That is a big payment. That is a Big Savior! What a gift Jesus has given you!

Because of Jesus, you have been forgiven and declared *not guilty*.

Because of Jesus, you can have peace and joy despite your circumstances.

Because of Jesus, you have an eternal home in Heaven with Him.

Because of Jesus, you have gone from a death sentence to a life of glory. Because of Jesus, you can be free.

In view of all this, Paul says that you are to offer your body as a living sacrifice, holy and pleasing to God. This is a lifestyle of wholehearted worship. And the result of worship is transformation.

Before you can change, the One who changes everything must capture your heart with His mercy and goodness. Meditate on His mercy, relish it, cherish it, embrace it, and respond to it with thanksgiving and praise. This will lead to worship in every part of your being.

Without the proper perspective of God's mercy, it is easy to lose sight of God's love. If that's the case for you, your path to experiencing change and transformation will be grueling.

2 Peter 1:3-11, NIV

His divine power has given us everything we need for a godly life through our knowledge of him who called us by his own glory and goodness. Through these he has given us his very great and precious promises, so that through them you may participate in the divine nature, having escaped the corruption in the world caused by evil desires.

For this very reason, make every effort to add to your faith goodness; and to goodness, knowledge; and to knowledge, self-control; and to self-control, perseverance; and to perseverance, godliness; and to godliness, mutual affection; and to mutual affection, love. For if you possess these qualities in increasing measure, they will keep you from being ineffective and unproductive in your knowledge of our Lord Jesus Christ. But whoever does not have them is nearsighted and blind, forgetting that they have been cleansed from their past sins.

Therefore, my brothers and sisters, make every effort to confirm your calling and election. For if you do these things, you will never stumble, and you will receive a rich welcome into the eternal kingdom of our Lord and Savior Jesus Christ.

If you don't apply spiritual growth to your Christian walk, you can become nearsighted and blind (2 Peter 1:9). The only kind of blindness that is worse than physical blindness is spiritual blindness. Spiritual blindness can be permanent if one does not recognize and *see* their need for Jesus. Helen Keller once said, "The only thing worse than being blind is having sight with no vision." This is what it means to be spiritually blind.

Not growing in God's Word keeps you in spiritual blindness. It makes you more susceptible to believe the ways of the world rather than the ways of God. The world says your body is your own. It saddens the heart of God and is a lie from the enemy (1 Corinthians 6:20). The Bible says that God formed you in your mother's womb (Psalm 139:13). In view of all God has done, your life is His. Your body is His. How you respond to the mercy of God will determine the level of transformation and change you will experience in your life.

A LIFE OF WORSHIP

Many people think attending a church service on Sunday morning and singing a few songs is all there is to worship. Though this may be one way to express worship, God views true worship as *how you live.*

A.W. Tozer wrote, "If you will not worship God seven days a week you do not worship Him on one day a week." When you worship God wholeheartedly you wake up every day thanking Him for all He has done. You offer all of your life to Him as a sacrifice for Him to use however He wants. It's a complete surrender of your will to God's. Worship is not just something done at church. It is not merely singing the words of a song. Worship is truly a lifestyle of thankfulness to God in and through the way you live. For that reason, it can be a battle.

Paul talks about this battle that wages in the mind. The way in which you're transformed, in fact, is when your mind is renewed. The battle is won when we reject the world's way of thinking and allow God to change our thoughts.

Many allow their feelings to influence their thoughts instead of allowing their thoughts to influence their feelings. Satan targets both your mind and your feelings, but if you let him have control of either, he will wreak havoc in your life. If you want to be transformed, you must replace the lies you have believed in your mind with the truth of God's Word. If you only follow your feelings, you are often following the same patterns of this world.

A friend once warned me that emotions are like a spinning roulette wheel. You never know which ones you are going to wake up to. If you follow your feelings instead of trusting in God's Word, then your life will seem like a spinning wheel of constantly changing emotion. It's exhausting and often detrimental to your life.

Instead, let God transform you into a new person by changing the way you think (Romans 12:2). Then you will learn God's good, perfect, and pleasing will for you. In some ways, this is the ultimate, "Let go and Let God" passage of Scripture. Let go of trying to transform yourself. Rather, let God transform you into a new person by changing the way you think. When He changes the way you think, it will change the way you act. Applying God's truth also leads to a grateful heart that learns to worship Him more completely.

The Holy Spirit will always guide you into truth. He will never direct you away from the will of God. And His will is that you know Him (John 17:3). When you do, you will worship Him accordingly. Your mind will choose to believe truth. Your actions will follow in love and gratitude. Feelings will follow as your heart is surrendered to the will and the Word of the Lord.

Knowledge alone never effectively changes anyone. Many people have biblical knowledge, but it does not always lead to action.

Change requires learning God's truth and applying it to your life. It requires thinking in new and better ways. Change depends on you relying on the Holy Spirit and tapping into God's power, rather than trusting in your own strength.

The essence of being a follower of Jesus is *following* Him! When you follow someone, you follow that person's lead. Do what they do. Say things they say. Obey their instructions. You allow them to train you. Over time, you become like them.

A friend to Encounter, Pastor Marty Walker, defines discipleship as *the process of becoming more like Jesus today than I was yesterday, and becoming more like Jesus tomorrow than I was today.* Discipleship is a process. It is a lifestyle and commitment. It is a labor of love and a reverent submission to the Lordship of Jesus Christ in your life every day. It is an all-in state of mind backed up by all-in actions. In other words, it is worship.

Being a Christian is one thing. Being a disciple is something altogether different. You can be a Christian but never be discipled. Discipleship is marked by spiritual growth. Without spiritual growth, it is difficult to live out your purpose. Some disciples don't mature simply because they refuse to go all in and love Jesus according to His definition of love. Jesus says that to love Him is to *obey* Him. God wants you to grow in your faith. He wants you to look like Jesus in word and deed.

Read, meditate, and journal the following scriptures.

Matthew 28:18-20, NIV

Then Jesus came to them and said, "All authority in heaven and on earth has been given to me. Therefore go and make disciples of all nations, baptizing them in the name of the Father and of the Son and of the Holy Spirit, and teaching them to obey everything I have commanded you. And surely I am with you always, to the very end of the age."

Luke 24:45, NIV

Then he opened their minds so they could understand the Scriptures.

John 13:35, NIV

"By this everyone will know that you are my disciples, if you love one another."

John 14:21, NIV

"Whoever has my commands and keeps them is the one who loves me. The one who loves me will be loved by my Father, and I too will love them and show myself to them."

Ephesians 4:22-24, NIV

You were taught, with regard to your former way of life, to put off your old self, which is being corrupted by its deceitful desires; to be made new in the attitude of your minds; and to put on the new self, created to be like God in true righteousness and holiness.

Ephesians 5:1-20, NIV

Follow God's example, therefore, as dearly loved children and walk in the way of love, just as Christ loved us and gave himself up for us as a fragrant offering and sacrifice to God. But among you there must not be even a hint of sexual immorality, or of any kind of impurity, or of greed, because these are improper for God's holy people. Nor should there be obscenity, foolish talk or coarse joking, which are out of place, but rather thanksgiving. For of this you can be sure: No immoral, impure or greedy person—such a person is an idolater—has any inheritance in the kingdom of Christ and of God. Let no one deceive you with empty words, for because of such things God's wrath comes on those who are disobedient. Therefore do not be partners with them.

For you were once darkness, but now you are light in the Lord. Live as children of light (for the fruit of the light consists in all goodness, righteousness and truth) and find out what pleases the Lord. Have nothing to do with the fruitless deeds of darkness, but rather expose them. It is shameful even to mention what the disobedient do in secret. But everything exposed by the light becomes visible—and everything that is illuminated becomes a light. This is why it is said: "Wake up, sleeper, rise from the dead, and Christ will shine on you."

Be very careful, then, how you live—not as unwise but as wise, making the most of every opportunity, because the days are evil. Therefore do not be foolish, but understand what the Lord's will is. Do not get drunk on wine, which leads to debauchery. Instead, be filled with the Spirit, speaking to one another with psalms, hymns, and songs from the Spirit. Sing and make music from your heart to the Lord, always giving thanks to God the Father for everything, in the name of our Lord Jesus Christ.

Philippians 4:8-9, NIV

Finally, brothers and sisters, whatever is true, whatever is noble, whatever is right, whatever is pure, whatever is lovely, whatever is admirable—if anything is excellent or praiseworthy—think about such things. Whatever you have learned or received or heard from me, or seen in me—put it into practice. And the God of peace will be with you.

1 John 2:3-6, NIV

We know that we have come to know him if we keep his commands. Whoever says, "I know him," but does not do what he commands is a liar, and the truth is not in that person. But if anyone obeys his word, love for God is truly made complete in them. This is how we know we are in him: Whoever claims to live in him must live as Jesus did.

PATHWAY TO TRANSFORMATION

Embrace discipleship by allowing God to transform you. Allow God to change you. Give God permission. It is our responsibility to renew our mind by applying God's truth to our lives. He won't just download the Bible into our brains. We must read it, learn it, and memorize it for it to transform us. No transformation can occur without it. Our job is to renew. His job is to transform.

If you allow God to give you a better way of thinking, you will discover a better way of living. Some people have said this renewing process is like re-wallpapering your mind. You have to strip the nasty old wallpaper from the walls of your mind and refresh it with a clean slate. Demolition has to take place.

2 Corinthians 10:5, NIV

We demolish arguments and every pretension that sets itself up against the knowledge of God, and we take captive every thought to make it obedient to Christ.

That's what re-wallpapering looks like. That is renewing your mind with God's truth; replacing lies that have been on the walls of your mind for far too long.

John 8:31-32, NIV

Jesus said, "If you hold to my teaching, you are really my disciples. Then you will know the truth, and the truth will set you free."

As a believer and follower of Jesus, you are no longer obligated to let the world influence your behavior. Christ has set you free from your old manner of life. That means that you can allow the Holy Spirit to guide you according to God's good, perfect, and pleasing will.

The Greek translation for *transformed* is "metamorphosis." The implication of this process is that the outside is transformed due to an inner work. Consider the way a caterpillar changes into what it was always meant to become, a butterfly. God never meant for it to remain a caterpillar. To become a beautiful butterfly, it must go through a time of transformation in the cocoon.

Likewise, those born into new life in Christ now have the nature of Christ within them. Now they must transform to become what the inner nature says they already are. As Christ followers, we must grow up so the nature of Christ within us can be seen.

2 Peter 3:18, NIV

But grow in the grace and knowledge of our Lord and Savior Jesus Christ. To him be glory both now and forever! Amen.

God doesn't want you to continue to crawl around in the muck and mire of your old life. He wants you to crawl into His arms and let the cocoon of His love transform you. It is what you are meant to do.

If you are willing to grow, God is willing to transform you. He can transform you into a new and beautiful creature that can be free.

BEING INTENTIONAL ABOUT GROWTH AND TRANSFORMATION

Transformation is not something to compartmentalize or put on a shelf periodically. You can't simply take it down when you feel like it. There is only one way to follow God—all-in. He wants your whole heart, your whole life. Consider this: If God is not Lord *of all* in your life, then He is not Lord *at all* in your life.

 ## Ask Yourself

What changes have I tried to make in my life in my own strength? How did that work out for me?

Considering what God has done for me, in what ways does my life reflect my gratitude to God?

How do I define worship?

PAUSE & PRAY

Write out your definition of worship and plan how you are going to worship God according to what you have learned in this lesson. Ask God to seal your plan with His Holy Spirit and ask others to hold you accountable to living it out.

Holy Spirit, show me how to offer my life, my mind, my body as a living and holy sacrifice that will worship You in spirit and in truth that is pleasing and acceptable. Reveal the changes You want to make that I confess I am not able to make in my own strength. As I continue to renew my mind to the truth of Your Word, transform my way of thinking and give me Your thoughts, Your counsel, Your wisdom, and Your power. In Jesus's name I pray.

Be sure to wait on the Lord after this prayer and journal what you hear.

⚓ ANCHOR 8

CHOOSE THE FREEDOM OF FORGIVENESS TO EXPERIENCE THE HEALING PEACE OF GOD.

Pray

As you begin this lesson, pray that you will have an Encounter with God as you earnestly seek Him. Don't rush through reading everything and don't rush through praying. Take some time to stop and listen so you may hear what God wants to say to you. Be sure to write whatever comes to your mind in your journal as you use the following as a prayer to the Lord:

Lord, I want to hear Your voice—and Your voice alone— through Your Word and throughout this lesson.

With every scripture or compilation of scriptures, pray these specific prayers:

Lord, what are You saying in Your Word?
Lord, what are You saying to me?
Lord, how do You want me to apply this to my life?

Journal everything that comes to your mind.

Make allowance for each other's faults, and forgive anyone who offends you. Remember, the Lord forgave you, so you must forgive others. Above all, clothe yourselves with love, which binds us all together in perfect harmony. And let the peace that comes from Christ rule in your hearts. For as members of one body you are called to live in peace. And always be thankful.

—Colossians 3:13-15, NLT

CHOOSING FORGIVENESS

The more you get to know God, the more you realize that His ways are starkly counter-cultural. His ways are always higher than our ways. One such area is forgiveness. When we place our trust in Jesus as Lord and Savior, He forgives our sins. Jesus instructs His followers to likewise forgive those who have sinned against them. We tend to be okay with being forgiven, but forgiving others is a bit more difficult to embrace.

In previous Anchor lessons, we discovered that God shows us incredible forgiveness. We learned that, in view of God's mercy, our lives should reflect our gratitude toward Him for all He has done for us. No matter what depraved sins we have committed, Jesus came to save and forgive us.

Read, meditate, and journal the following passages of Scripture:

John 3:16-17, NIV

"For God so loved the world that he gave his one and only Son, that whoever believes in him shall not perish but have eternal life. For God did not send his Son into the world to condemn the world, but to save the world through him."

Psalm 103, NIV

Praise the LORD, my soul; all my inmost being, praise his holy name. Praise the LORD, my soul, and forget not all his benefits—who forgives all your sins and heals all your diseases, who redeems your life from the pit and crowns you with love and compassion, who satisfies your desires with good things so that your youth is renewed like the eagle's. The LORD works righteousness and justice for all the oppressed. He made known his ways to Moses, his deeds to the people of Israel: The LORD is compassionate and gracious, slow to anger, abounding in love. He will not always accuse, nor will he harbor his anger forever; he does not treat us as our sins deserve or repay us according to our iniquities. For as high as the heavens are above the earth, so great is his love for those who fear him; as far as the east is from the west, so far has he removed our transgressions from us. As a father has compassion on his children, so the LORD has compassion on those who fear him; for he knows how we are formed, he remembers that we are dust. The life of mortals is like grass, they flourish like a flower of the field; the wind blows over it and it is gone, and its place remembers it no more. But from everlasting to everlasting the LORD love is with those who fear him and his righteousness with their children's children—with those who keep his covenant and remember to obey his precepts. The LORD has established his throne in heaven, and his kingdom rules over all. Praise the LORD, you his angels, you mighty ones who do his bidding, who obey his word. Praise the LORD, all his heavenly hosts, you his servants who do his will. Praise the LORD, all his works everywhere in his dominion.

Praise the LORD, my soul.

Romans 5:6-11, NIV

You see, at just the right time, when we were still powerless, Christ died for the ungodly. Very rarely will anyone die for a righteous person, though for a good person someone might possibly dare to die. But God demonstrates his own love for us in this: While we were still sinners, Christ died for us.

Since we have now been justified by his blood, how much more shall we be saved from God's wrath through him! For if, while we were God's enemies, we were reconciled to him through the death of his Son, how much more, having been reconciled, shall we be saved through his life! Not only is this so, but we also boast in God through our Lord Jesus Christ, through whom we have now received reconciliation.

Colossians 3:13-15, NLT (Anchor 8's key verse)

Make allowance for each other's faults, and forgive anyone who offends you. Remember, the Lord forgave you, so you must forgive others. Above all, clothe yourselves with love, which binds us all together in perfect harmony. And let the peace that comes from Christ rule in your hearts. For as members of one body you are called to live in peace. And always be thankful.

Matthew 6:9-13, NIV

"This, then, is how you should pray: Our Father in heaven, hallowed be your name, your kingdom come, your will be done, on earth as it is in heaven. Give us today our daily bread. And forgive us our debts, as we also have forgiven our debtors. And lead us not into temptation, but deliver us from the evil one."

With this instruction on how to pray, Jesus teaches us that our lives should reflect the same kind of forgiveness we have received. The focus of this anchor is not on how to *pray* (Anchors 10 and 11 will focus on that). But if we want to have peace with God, we must heed the key statements in the Lord's prayer that show us how to *live*.

Jesus wants us to be sincere and humble. He wants us to be real and authentic. He desires for our hearts to be right with others and with Him. To fully understand this, let's dig deeper into what Jesus went on to say about forgiveness.

Matthew 6:14-15, NIV

"For if you forgive other people when they sin against you, your heavenly Father will also forgive you. But if you do not forgive others their sins, your Father will not forgive your sins."

Jesus said we should ask God to forgive us in the same way that we have forgiven others. Think about that. It means you can't go halfway in forgiveness. God doesn't forgive you halfway. It means you can't hold a grudge against someone or hold onto the offense. God doesn't hold onto all the egregious things you have done to Him when He forgives you. It means that every sin committed against you is forgivable. God forgives everyone who asks for His forgiveness, regardless of how bad the sin was.

Jesus says "follow Me." Everything He calls us to do, He did first. Jesus was treated in the most depraved manner anyone could ever be treated. He was mocked and beaten. His skin was torn from His body. He was nailed to a cross even though He was innocent. He was even taunted as He hung on the cross. Even so, His love caused Him to say, "Father, forgive them, for they do not know what they are doing" (Luke 23:34, NIV). If He can forgive like that, He can certainly give you the ability to forgive others, even those you may consider unforgivable.

Isaiah 53:5-6, NIV

But he was pierced for our transgressions, he was crushed for our iniquities; the punishment that brought us peace was on him, and by his wounds we are healed. We all, like sheep, have gone astray, each of us has turned to our own way; and the Lord has laid on him the iniquity of us all.

WHY IT IS CRUCIAL TO OFFER COMPLETE FORGIVENESS

Pastor John Wesley told a story about a man who came to him and said, "I will never forgive." Wesley replied, "Then I hope you never sin!"

He knew that Jesus's instruction to follow Him included forgiving others as He had forgiven them. We all need what we don't want to give—forgiveness.

Mark 11:22-25, NIV

"Have faith in God," Jesus answered. "Truly I tell you, if anyone says to this mountain, 'Go, throw yourself into the sea,' and does not doubt in their heart but believes that what they say will happen, it will be done for them. Therefore I tell you, whatever you ask for in prayer, believe that you have received it, and it will be yours. And when you stand praying, if you hold anything against anyone, forgive them, so that your Father in heaven may forgive you your sins."

Recovering effectively from any hurt in life requires obedience in the matter of forgiveness. Jesus teaches that faith in God gives you power and authority for dealing with difficult things in your life. **He also tags forgiveness as a component of this equation.** That is because He is interested in your complete healing. He wants you to overcome the difficult mountains in your life—hurts, habits, sins. Forgiveness is a necessary ingredient for freedom.

1 John 2:9-11, NIV

Anyone who claims to be in the light but hates a brother or sister is still in the darkness. Anyone who loves their brother and sister lives in the light, and there is nothing in them to make them stumble. But anyone who hates a brother or sister is in the darkness and walks around in the darkness. They do not know where they are going, because the darkness has blinded them.

Unforgiveness will keep you in the dark. It will prevent you from experiencing peace. It will keep you from being in the will of God; in fact, unforgiveness has the potential to destroy you.

A resentful heart traps you in a dysfunctional cycle of sin and defeat. When you are angry, bitter, resentful, and unforgiving toward someone, you are only hurting yourself. As you replay the offense over and over in your mind, you create mental and spiritual anguish.

Resentment can also cause serious health issues. Your stomach can feel the ill effects of swallowing bitterness. It can become like a cancer that eats you alive. Resentment is an emotional poison with spiritual and physical consequences. It leaks into your soul and can lead to depression, stress, fatigue, joint pain, back pain, stomach problems, and other potentially serious diseases.

Chances are high that the person you are refusing to forgive is oblivious to the turmoil you're experiencing. The person you are allowing to continue to hurt you may even be dead—but living rent free in your mind! It's time to evict the offender by forgiving them, thereby freeing your life of their damaging effect.

Resentment cannot change the past. It rarely even hurts the person who hurt you and never makes you feel any better. Have you ever known anyone to say, "I feel so much better carrying around this bitterness?"

Proverbs 17:22, NIV

A cheerful heart is good medicine, but a crushed spirit dries up the bones.

Resentment can make you toxic. It can lead you to gossip. It can make you skeptical or create a critical spirit or entitled mindset. It can destroy relationships. It can destroy families. It can destroy businesses. It can destroy ministries and churches. Resentment is a trick and a tool that Satan uses to destroy.

When you choose to forgive others the way Jesus forgives, you choose freedom. The path may be difficult, but it is good. Jesus is intent upon reconciling you to God. When you follow His commands, one of the amazing benefits is that He reconciles you to others as well.

WHAT IS FORGIVENESS?

What exactly is forgiveness? You may have heard many opinions and thoughts on the subject, some true and others false. Let's consider what forgiveness is and is not:

- **Forgiveness is not forgetting.** Forgiving someone doesn't mean agreeing that what they did was no big deal. It was a big deal. It hurt. To shrug it away or deny it is dishonest. Hurts can leave scars. You may never forget a wrong, but you don't have to be paralyzed by it. When God says He does not remember your sins, it's not because He has amnesia. He is simply telling you that He does not hold your past sins against you—or over you. God releases the debt of your sin. Although you may not forget the hurt, to forgive, you must release the debt.

- **Forgiveness is a choice.** Some people hold onto their anger in an attempt to protect themselves against further hurt. Others may want revenge for what was done to them. They withhold forgiveness hoping the other person will somehow feel as much pain as they caused. These people only bring themselves more pain.

   Instead, allow God to work in the other person's life. That is His job, not yours. Let the person off your hook. As long as you refuse to forgive them, you are still hooked to them. You are chained to your past, bound up in bitterness. By forgiving, you free yourself and trust that God will deal with them justly and fairly. You may say, "But you don't know how much this person hurt me!" Although that is true, Jesus knows. And He has instructed you to forgive others *for your own good*. Until you let go of your bitterness, that person is still hurting you. You cannot change or fix the past, but you can be free from its negative effects. There's an old saying, "To forgive is to set a captive free and realize that you were the captive." You must choose to obey God and leave the consequences to Him.

- **Forgiveness means giving up your right to get even.** To forgive, you have to reject any thought or act of revenge. This doesn't mean you continue to put up with abusive behavior. God does not tolerate sin, and neither should you. If anyone treats you in an abusive manner, you need to set up scriptural boundaries to protect yourself. You are instructed to forgive, but you are not instructed to stay in abusive situations. Allow God to handle what was done to you by saying, "In view of what God has done for me, I have no right to hold on to this offense. I'm releasing this person to God. I'm giving up my right to get even."

THE PARABLE OF THE UNMERCIFUL SERVANT

Matthew 18:21-35, NIV

Then Peter came to Jesus and asked, "Lord, how many times shall I forgive my brother or sister who sins against me? Up to seven times?" Jesus answered, "I tell you, not seven times, but seventy-seven times. "Therefore, the kingdom of heaven is like a king who wanted to settle accounts with his servants. As he began the settlement, a man who owed him ten thousand bags of gold was brought to him. Since he was not able to pay, the master ordered that he and his wife and his children and all that he had be sold to repay the debt.

"At this the servant fell on his knees before him. 'Be patient with me,' he begged, 'and I will pay back everything.' The servant's master took pity on him, canceled the debt and let him go. "But when that servant went out, he found one of his fellow servants who owed him a hundred silver coins. He grabbed him and began to choke him. 'Pay back what you owe me!' he demanded.

"His fellow servant fell to his knees and begged him, 'Be patient with me, and I will pay it back.' "But he refused. Instead, he went off and had the man thrown into prison until he could pay the debt. When the other servants saw what had happened, they were outraged and went and told their master everything that had happened.

"Then the master called the servant in. 'You wicked servant,' he said, 'I canceled all that debt of yours because you begged me to. Shouldn't you have had mercy on your fellow servant just as I had on you?' In anger his master handed him over to the jailers to be tortured, until he should pay back all he owed. "This is how my heavenly Father will treat each of you unless you forgive your brother or sister from your heart."

This doesn't mean you should keep count of offenses against you. It means the opposite. You are to keep on forgiving, even when the offenses against you are immeasurable. Forgiveness is an infinite principle. When you forgive, as Jesus has commanded, you will be blessed beyond measure.

Notice how Jesus described the unmerciful servant. He owed 10,000 talents to a king. It was an enormous sum to repay (one talent was equivalent to seventeen years of wages). The king wanted to settle all outstanding accounts, so he ordered that the man, his wife and children, and everything he owned to be sold. The servant fell on his knees and asked his master for mercy. The king forgave all his debt.

You would think that, in view of his master's mercy, this man would show that same mercy to others. But he found a fellow servant who owed him one hundred denarii (only three months of wages) and demanded payment. The debt his fellow servant owed did not compare to the massive debt from which the king had forgiven him. But when the servant fell to his knees and begged for mercy, the unmerciful man refused. He threw the servant in jail until he could pay off the debt. It did not end well for the unmerciful servant.

Forgiveness doesn't change the consequences of another person's sin. You only have to look at the sin of Adam and Eve to know that we suffer consequences from other people's choices. You can't change the past. It happened. The choice now is whether you will choose the freedom of forgiveness or stay in the bondage of bitterness.

Reconciliation and trust need time to be rebuilt if they can be rebuilt at all. Forgiving someone is necessary. Trusting them again is optional and requires discernment. Trust can only be rebuilt by trustworthy actions, not merely words. When two people surrender to God and choose forgiveness, it is possible to rebuild and restore trust in time. In a perfect world, reconciliation would always be the end result of forgiveness. However, forgiveness and reconciliation are two different things. It is possible to completely forgive someone and not be reconciled to that person. You may forgive people that have done unspeakable things to you but, if they are still dangerous or toxic to your life, reconciliation will not be possible.

Others in your life may have bankrupted your trust account. If you are ever to be in relationship with them again, they will need to earn your trust by making deposits in the relationship. This requires right motives and trustworthy behavior. You must forgive them, but trust can only be rebuilt with consistent and worthy deposits of love and grace. It often takes time and patience. If both parties are willing, it can be done. However, if one party does not have right motives, it is best to not allow them to take up physical or mental space in your life. Forgive them, love them, and release them to God.

CLOSING OUR ACCOUNTS WITH OTHERS

Colossians 3:12-15, NLT

Since God chose you to be the holy people he loves, you must clothe yourselves with tenderhearted mercy, kindness, humility, gentleness, and patience. Make allowance for each other's faults, and forgive anyone who offends you. Remember, the Lord forgave you, so you must forgive others. Above all, clothe yourselves with love, which binds us all together in perfect harmony. And let the peace that comes from Christ rule in your hearts. For as members of one body you are called to live in peace. And always be thankful.

Jesus doesn't want you to have unsettled accounts with people. He doesn't want unforgiveness to create distance. Settling your accounts means canceling the debts you owe others and the debts they owe you. You readily offer and accept forgiveness.

There are times when forgiveness is not just a matter between you and others. Forgiveness can be something you need to offer to yourself. People often can't forgive themselves for something in the past. They feel like they don't deserve forgiveness. They sometimes punish themselves for their past by allowing it to hold them hostage.

Forgiving yourself means accepting the truth that God has already forgiven you. You have to choose to believe what God has done for you is true. Because it is true, you can extend that same forgiveness to yourself. Allow your misplaced shame and guilt to be lifted away by God.

In some instances, people can also be mad at God for things that have happened to them in their life. That may even be the case for you. God already knows if you have been disappointed or if you are mad at Him. He is big enough to handle your grievances against Him. No matter how misplaced your perceptions or expectations of Him may have been (or still are), God has never sinned against you. He does not need your forgiveness. Nevertheless, in view of His mercy toward you, you may need to let go of your disappointments for what He did (or did not do) in your life.

To be completely free from resentment, shame, and guilt, you need to choose forgiveness in every area of your life. If you do not, any spiritual growth from hurt, addiction, or character defaults will come to a halt. You will not be able to move forward to a life of freedom. **Forgiveness is the key to your restoration and peace.** It takes courage and honesty.

Revealing the truth that you have been hurt or are being hurt by another person is critical to healing. You can't get over pain until you admit its presence in your life. To close the door on the past, you have to admit what happened, reveal that it was wrong, and identify why it hurt you. Finally, you have to forgive the person who hurt you.

Don't make the mistake of waiting for the other person to ask for forgiveness. That may never happen. They may be clueless that they hurt you or callous to the pain they caused. They may not even be alive today. In any case, Jesus did not wait for those who were crucifying Him to apologize before He forgave them. While on the cross, Jesus prayed, "Father, forgive them, they do not know what they are doing" (Luke 23:34, NIV).

Ultimately, forgiveness is not about the other person. It's about experiencing freedom from the bitterness that unforgiveness brings.

Don't wait until you feel like forgiving. Make the hard choice to forgive now, even if you don't feel like it. Once you choose to forgive, Satan will lose his hold on you and God can begin to heal your damaged emotions. Forgive from the heart or the process won't work. It must come from a sincere place, not something to check off a to-do list.

For many who have been a victim of sexual abuse, physical abuse, childhood abuse, neglect, or abandonment, what was done to you was so wrong. It hurts the very heart of God. It's difficult to comprehend that kind of pain. Nothing will ever make what was done right or okay, but you will not find peace and freedom from your offenders until you are able to forgive them. Forgiving them does not excuse them for the harm they caused. It will, however, release you from the power they have over you. So, leave it at the foot of the cross. Give it to God.

 ## Ask Yourself

How can I close all my accounts with other people?

How can I become a peacemaker?

To move forward and choose the freedom of forgiveness, spend time slowly working through the following activity:

- Ask God to forgive you for withholding forgiveness toward any person.

- Ask Him to reveal every person you need to forgive. Make a list of people God brings to mind. If needed, remember to include yourself on that list.

- Say, "Lord, I choose to forgive _____ and what he/she did to me."

- For each name on the list, write out what they did to hurt you; name the offense. (When sharing this with others, please note that you don't have to mention the names of people on your list.)

- Reveal the hurt and acknowledge the pain. Think about what God has done with your sin and let Him touch your heart.

- Release the offender. You will know that you have fully released an offender when you can pray for God's blessing on their lives. You might not be able to forget, but you can forgive.

- Say an honest prayer, "God, I release (name of my offender) to You. I humbly ask You to bless their life."

- Finally, close all accounts with other people in your life. Whom have you hurt? Do you need to offer an apology to anyone and ask for their forgiveness? Name those people and pray for God to guide you in asking for their forgiveness. Sometimes, it may not be possible. Those people may not be around, or it may not be beneficial to have a conversation with them because it could cause further harm. In such a case, you can place an empty chair in front of you and act as if they are in that chair. Say your apologies and ask God to give you peace in the situation. Ask Him to cleanse your heart and bless the person that you hurt.

If you are working through *Encounter* on your own, talk with a trusted individual about what you've learned and experienced from this activity. If you are meeting with a study group, give each person up to five minutes to share as much as possible from this exercise. Once everyone has had an opportunity to share, a second round of sharing may be allowed if there is time to do so. If you need more time, please reach out to a fellow member of your study to schedule a time to further share how you responded.

Anchor 9

ALLOW GOD'S WORD TO BECOME THE AUTHORITY OVER MY LIFE.

Pray

As you begin this lesson, pray that you will have an Encounter with God as you earnestly seek Him. Don't rush through reading everything and don't rush through praying. Take some time to stop and listen so you may hear what God wants to say to you. Be sure to write whatever comes to your mind in your journal as you use the following as a prayer to the Lord:

Lord, I want to hear Your voice—and Your voice alone—through Your Word and throughout this lesson.

With every scripture or compilation of scriptures, pray these specific prayers:

Lord, what are You saying in Your Word?
Lord, what are You saying to me?
Lord, how do You want me to apply this to my life?

Journal everything that comes to your mind.

All Scripture is inspired by God and is useful to teach us what is true and make us realize what is wrong in our lives. It corrects us when we are wrong and teaches us to do what is right. God uses it to prepare and equip His people to do every good work.
—2 Timothy 3:16-17, NLT

WHO HAS THE FINAL SAY?

At Encounter, we believe that the Bible is true, inspired by God, and holds authority over our lives. God loves us so much that He wants us to know Him. That's why He gave us a road map, His Word. Only God could have been so kind as to have left us with an eternal love letter.

Within Scripture, God reveals Himself to us. He shows us how we can be forgiven and reconciled to Him. He instructs us how to live a godly life. He encourages and guides us. God's Word gives us wisdom, peace, and joy. It equips us to serve with love and purpose.

Knowing God's Word will separate those anchored in the love of Christ from lukewarm or double-minded people. You must allow God's Word to become the authority over your life.

Most people find themselves in one of three camps in their spiritual life when it comes to knowing and following God's Word:

1. They either don't believe God's Word or flat out ignore and reject it.

2. They think they are a good person and try to do the best they can in their own strength.

3. They believe God's Word and pursue His truth in their daily living.

The definition of the word "authority" in *Webster's Dictionary* is, "Power to influence or command thought, opinion or behavior." Taking that at face value, allowing God's Word to become the authority over your life means looking to Scripture as the ultimate source of power to influence your thought, opinions, and behavior. It means that you believe and agree with what the Bible says and, as such, your life reflects obedience to the truth of God's Word. It means yielding your thoughts and will to the higher and better thoughts of God. It means that your response to God's love for you would be to gratefully love Him back. Think about which camp most accurately describes your choices.

Why is it so important to follow God's truth in all areas of life? Every self-defeating behavior is the result of a lie that you believed. Every stronghold that has taken root began with a lie. Until you get to know the God of the Bible, you will never learn the truth that sets you free.

John 14:6, NIV

Jesus answered, "I am the way and the truth and the life. No one comes to the Father except through me."

Jesus didn't say He knew the way or that He could point the way or that He was only one of many ways to the Father. He didn't say He knew the truth or had the truth. He didn't say that He simply taught the truth. Jesus said, "I *am* the way, and the truth, and the life."

We live in a society of subjective ideas and competing opinions. Sometimes, just because a thought comes into a person's mind, they decide it is their reality. Feelings, perceptions, or attitudes tend to translate into a mindset of "to each their own." Many have views that differ dramatically from the truths that are in God's Word. In fact, Jesus addressed the tendency man has to follow his own thoughts and reject God's Word.

Mark 7:8-9, NIV

"You have let go of the commands of God and are holding on to human traditions." And he continued, "You have a fine way of setting aside the commands of God in order to observe your own traditions!"

Jesus was speaking to the Pharisees about their zeal for legalistic observances. He knew that the crux of their rebellion was a heart matter. The same holds true for us. We like to put our own interpretations on Scripture as it suits us. We like to pick and choose what we want to follow and push the rest aside.

Proverbs 14:12, NIV

There is a way that appears to be right, but in the end it leads to death.

The words of Proverbs 14:12 are repeated in Proverbs 16:25. It's safe to say that God knew we would prefer to follow our sinful nature. Perhaps that is why He inspired these words of wisdom to be written in the Bible more than once. When things are repeated in God's Word, it is wise to pay attention.

2 Timothy 3:16, NLT

All Scripture is inspired by God and is useful to teach us what is true and to make us realize what is wrong in our lives. It corrects us when we are wrong and teaches us to do what is right. God uses it to prepare and equip his people to do every good work.

Who and what you believe can influence your life more than most anything else. If you believe God's Word, your life and choices will reflect that. If you don't, your life will be a series of poor choices.

Hosea 4:6, NIV

"My people are destroyed from lack of knowledge."

When Hosea wrote these words from God, His people and even the priests had looked to false gods. They had not believed Him or allowed His laws to be their authority. As a result, their destruction was imminent. If we do not heed the warning, the same could be true of us.

Dr. Charles Stanley once said that conviction is something we are so completely convinced is true that we will take a stand for it regardless of the consequence. A preference, on the other hand, is a belief that could change under certain conditions.

Isaiah 66:2, NIV

Has not my hand made all these things, and so they came into being?" declares the Lord. "These are the ones I look on with favor: those who are humble and contrite in spirit, and who tremble at my word.

A healthy understanding of God's Word creates awe and respect for the Scriptures and the One who gave them to us. Everyone must make the life impacting choice of whether they will live by convictions or by preferences. One leads to life. The other leads to death.

Isaiah 40:8, NIV

The grass withers and the flowers fall, but the word of our God endures forever.

Isaiah 55:11, NIV

"so is my word that goes out from my mouth: It will not return to me empty, but will accomplish what I desire and achieve the purpose for which I sent it."

Matthew 24:35, NIV

"Heaven and earth will pass away, but my words will never pass away."

God's Word stands the test of time. It is eternal. Culture changes, but God never changes. He never becomes outdated or irrelevant. Nothing in God's Word is void of meaning or relevance. To know God is to know His Word. To love God is to obey His Word.

John 16:13, NIV

"But when he, the Spirit of truth, comes, he will guide you into all the truth. He will not speak on his own; he will speak only what he hears, and he will tell you what is yet to come."

The Holy Spirit lives in Christ followers and guides them into truth. As a person led by God, you must yield to His guidance and truth.

Psalm 119, ESV

Take time to read Psalm 119 throughout this week. This is the longest chapter in the Bible, but it is also one of the most encouraging. The psalmist focuses on the many benefits of God's Word. He had experienced how important it is to recognize the blessing of knowing and following Scripture. This chapter contains so many nuggets of wisdom. The following are just a few that can equip you in life:

119:9—How can a young man keep his way pure? By living according to Your Word.

119:11—I have hidden Your Word in my heart that I might not sin against You.

119:89—Your Word, Lord, is eternal; it stands firm in the heavens.

119:105—Your Word is a lamp to my feet and a light to my path.

119:114—You are my refuge and my shield; I have put my hope in Your Word.

119:133—Direct my footsteps according to Your Word; let no sin rule over me.

119:160—All Your words are true; all your righteous laws are eternal.

Psalm 19:7-11, NIV

The law of the Lord is perfect, refreshing the soul. The statutes of the Lord are trustworthy, making wise the simple. The precepts of the Lord are right, giving joy to the heart.

The commands of the Lord are radiant, giving light to the eyes. The fear of the Lord is pure, enduring forever. The decrees of the Lord are firm, and all of them are righteous. They are more precious than gold, than much pure gold; they are sweeter than honey, than honey from the honeycomb. By them your servant is warned; in keeping them there is great reward.

The phrase, "the law of the Lord" is a Hebrew term used to describe Scripture. Some translations even say, "the instructions of the Lord." The Bible is full of amazing benefits. It is the Word of life.

Reflecting upon the above verses, we see that God's Word is perfect. Nothing needs to be added to it or taken away. What's more, as society and culture changes, you don't have to change what you know to be true. You can stand on the firm foundation of God's Word.

God's Word also gives wisdom. You don't have to be a scholar or theologian to understand it. The trustworthiness of God's Word can make even the simpleminded wise (Psalm 19:7). That's good news! When you read and believe God's Word, His Holy Spirit does the work of illuminating the truth.

Hebrews 4:12, NLT

The Word of God is alive and powerful. It is sharper than the sharpest two-edged sword, cutting between soul and spirit, between joint and marrow. It exposes our innermost thoughts and desires.

God's Word is living power that will change your life if you believe it, apply it to your life, and trust God for the results. Ultimately, success or failure for the Christ follower depends on how much of the Bible you get into your heart and how obedient you are to it. If you are not applying the Word of God to your life, you are setting yourself up for a fall.

John 8:31-32, NIV

To the Jews who had believed Him, Jesus said, "If you hold to My teaching, you are really My disciples. Then you will know the truth and the truth will set you free."

If you are going to be a true disciple of Jesus Christ, you need to get into the Word of God so the Word of God can get into you. When God's Word is believed and perceived as truth, it becomes the authority over your life. Change requires learning the truth. People often think they are accurately quoting the above Scripture when they say, "The truth will set you free." If you read it closely, you will note that these words are only a portion of what Jesus said. People repeat the second part of John 8:32 and take it out of context. However, if you are not submitted to the truth of God, then it will probably make you miserable, angry, and confused. Truth, alone, never sets anyone free.

Knowing and following Jesus, applying His truth to your life, is the key to freedom. By submitting and surrendering your life to Him, you are agreeing to make the Bible the authority over every single issue in your life. You can't be submitted to Jesus and not be submitted to God's Word. Making Jesus and God's Word the authority over your life allows you to have the peace of God and experience the blessings of God in your life. You will have trials and temptations in this world, but you never have to face them alone. God will help carry you through everything you face in this life.

TIME TO DECIDE

You have a decision to make in Anchor 9. You can acknowledge it and even agree with it, but it requires something more. You must make God's Word the authority over every issue, every matter, every event, and every decision that you will face from this day forward.

Nobody else can study God's Word for you. It must be your decision to passionately pursue Him. You pursue that which you prize. In other words, when something is a priority in your life, you will chase it with abandon. To attain the prize, your old patterns and former ways of living in this world must be replaced by new ways of living. The lies of this world must be replaced by the truth of God's Word.

Wisdom is seeing life from God's perspective. In other words, it is not enough to think about Scripture, you have to think *scripturally*. When you start seeing life from God's perspective, you start putting into practice that which you are learning. God's Word, if left sitting on a shelf, will not transform you. The truth has to penetrate your heart.

We learn far more by doing than by hearing. It has been said that people retain about ten percent of what they hear, twenty percent of what they see, and ninety percent of what they do.

James 1:22-25, NIV

Do not merely listen to the Word, and so deceive yourselves. Do what it says. Anyone who listens to the Word but does not do what it says is like a man who looks at his face in the mirror and, after looking at himself, goes away and immediately forgets what he looks like. But the man who looks intently into the perfect law that gives freedom, and continues to do this, not forgetting what he has heard, but doing it—he will be blessed in what he does.

Nike wasn't the first to say, "Just do it." It seems the idea has always been in the Bible. So, how will you respond? Will you allow God's Word to become the authority over your life?

Just do it, and God will do the rest.

Ask Yourself

Which one of the three spiritual camps best identifies my behavior and choices? Do I need to change camps? What would I need to do differently in order to change camps?

Do I live by convictions or by preferences? How will the difference affect my life?

What lies have I believed that have led to self-destructive behaviors, patterns, or strongholds in my life?

What is keeping me from allowing God's Word to become the authority over my life?

Anchor 10

COMMIT TO A DAILY PRAYER LIFE AND GROW MY RELATIONSHIP WITH THE FATHER.

Pray

As you begin this lesson, pray that you will have an Encounter with God as you earnestly seek Him. Don't rush through reading everything and don't rush through praying. Take some time to stop and listen so you may hear what God wants to say to you. Be sure to write whatever comes to your mind in your journal as you use the following as a prayer to the Lord:

Lord, I want to hear Your voice—and Your voice alone—through Your Word and throughout this lesson.

With every scripture or compilation of scriptures, pray these specific prayers:

Lord, what are You saying in Your Word?
Lord, what are You saying to me?
Lord, how do You want me to apply this to my life?

Journal everything that comes to your mind.

Be joyful always; pray continually; give thanks in all circumstances, for this is God's will for you in Christ Jesus.

—1 Thessalonians 5:16-18, ESV

PRACTICING PRAYER

At Encounter, our prayer is that you will follow God and live a transformed life of freedom and peace. In fact, Anchor 10 is all about prayer. It is our way to seek God and trust Him for the results. The purpose is to know God by spending time with Him, waiting to hear from Him, being in His presence, and trusting Him. Jesus did all these things.

During His ministry on earth, Jesus spent much time in prayer. He was purposeful and needed to get away and be alone with God. He needed to be in God's presence. Jesus needed the power of prayer to spend time talking to His Father. If Jesus, the Son of God, needed that to accomplish His mission here on earth, imagine how much more intentional we should be about seeking God through prayer and growing our relationship with our Father in Heaven?

Becoming more like Jesus does not happen naturally; it happens supernaturally. Only when we have a surrendered heart can we expect to know God's heart in this way.

Scripture is full of examples, instruction, and wisdom about prayer.

Psalm 50:15, NASB

"Call upon Me in the day of trouble and I will rescue you."

Who do you call when you are in trouble?
Do you go to the throne, or do you go to the phone?

James 5:13, NIV

Is anyone among you in trouble? Let them pray.

Anchor 10

With such clear and beneficial instructions, why do others rarely call upon God when trouble comes? Or why is it that we only call upon God in times of trouble, but don't bother to spend time with Him on a regular basis? There could be a variety of reasons, but one is simply that we have wrong motives. Our motives have a direct correlation to the effectiveness of our prayers.

James 4:2-3, NIV

You desire but do not have, so you kill. You covet but you cannot get what you want, so you quarrel and fight. You do not have because you do not ask God. When you ask, you do not receive, because you ask with wrong motives, that you may spend what you get on your pleasures.

Let's explore some biblical foundations for prayer, so you can learn to come boldly to God with faith and confidence, with right motives, knowing that He hears your prayers and answers them in His good and perfect way.

God had you in mind when He created the universe and formed you in your mother's womb. He wants to be in a loving relationship with you. He wants to spend time with you, and prayer is the pathway for that. When you quiet your busy life through prayer, you learn to be in God's presence. You begin listening to Him, waiting on Him, trusting in Him, surrendering to Him, believing Him, and running after Him with all your heart. You get to experience God's best plan for you. When you spend time with God in prayer, you are not so consumed by the things of this world. You become less consumed with selfish desires. Spending time in prayer with God will change you. It will allow you to know God better. It will help you more readily follow His will. It will cause you to be more concerned about God's *presence* than His *presents*.

When you decide to spend time with God in prayer, He gives clarity. You begin to see that nothing in your life is hidden from Almighty God. He sees all and knows all. Your secrets are not secrets to Him. When you get honest in prayer, an atmosphere is created that is more conducive to peace and healing.

CAN MY PRAYERS BE HINDERED?

Isaiah 1:15-17, BSB

"When you spread out your hands in prayer, I will hide My eyes from you; even if you offer many prayers, I will not listen. Your hands are full of blood; wash and make yourselves clean. Take your evil deeds out of my sight! Stop doing wrong, learn to do right."

Psalm 66:18-20, NIV

If I had cherished sin in my heart, the Lord would not have listened; but God has surely listened and heard my voice in prayer. Praise be to God, who has not rejected my prayer or withheld His love from me!

We do not approach God in prayer on our own good merits. We approach Him only by His amazing grace. We cannot approach God in prayer because we are good or have done good works. We can approach Him because of the finished work of Christ that has already been done on our behalf. The work of Jesus bridges the separation that exists between the sins of humankind and the God who created humankind.

When a person recognizes and believes in the finished work of Jesus, those sins no longer have any room in the Christ follower's life. This means that willful, deliberate, and repetitive sin hinders your prayers because it hinders your relationship with God.

Should you expect God to answer your prayers faithfully when you are not faithful to believe, follow, and honor Him? If you know the nature of God, you know His grace is an abundant gift. It shouldn't be cheapened. God cannot be mocked. He doesn't play games. He waits patiently for you to honestly come to Him.

Being honest with God about your sins, repenting from them, and asking for forgiveness will close that gap. By doing so, your prayers may be heard by God and answered according to His good and perfect will.

Satan, on the other hand, wants to keep you separated from God. He doesn't want you to be in an honest, fulfilling relationship with your Father. He doesn't want you to have God's peace and power. He wants to distract you so there's no time to pray. However, it all goes back to choosing God's truth over Satan's deceit. (You will learn how to fight these lies through prayer in Anchor 11.)

Hebrews 4:16, NLT

"So let us come boldly to the throne of our gracious God. There we will receive His mercy, and we will find grace to help us when we need it most.

Jeremiah 33:3, GNT

"Call to Me, and I will answer you; I will tell you wonderful and marvelous things that you know nothing about."

A good, honest relationship is built on dialogue between two parties. In the same way, prayer has all the characteristics of a deeply meaningful conversation between two people. When it's between you and God, the result can be even more wonderful. Prayer allows us to know God better and experience more of His love. It makes us grateful and hungry to remain in close relationship with Him. Communicating with God, both by speaking *and* listening, is the only way to build a relationship. And there is no more exciting experience than encountering that kind of love between the Father and His child.

Jeremiah 29:13, NIV

"You will seek Me and find Me when you seek Me with all your heart."

What a promise! Wouldn't it be such a joy to experience the full blessings of it? It is possible, otherwise God wouldn't have included it in His Word.

King David sought the Lord with his whole heart. He wrote many psalms that were prayers. Sometimes he was happy, other times he was heartbroken. Some of his words are filled with gratitude and others with lament. In all of the psalms he wrote, he was honest with God. He spoke, listened, and heard from God. They had a real relationship that was unique to the two of them. That is how your relationship with God is intended to be—honest, real, and personal.

Nothing will build your relationship with Jesus Christ like a committed prayer life. It is the life breath of communication with Him. What a privilege it is to have this connection to Heaven. The lines should always be open.

Prayer gives our battles over to God and allows Him to fight for us. It lays our burdens at the foot of the cross. Prayer gives us proper perspective. It tells our problems how big God is instead of telling God how big our problems are. Prayer reminds us that our God has great power and that we are powerless without Him.

While prayer is a personal means of being in relationship with God, you will never impress Him with fancy religious words. He can see right through insincere prayers. True prayer gives God the reverence He deserves. So, treating Him like another "buddy" would be naive. There should be a balance of faith, boldness, and awe that comes with being in a relationship with the God that created you.

One of God's greatest presents to you is allowing you to be in His presence. Since prayer is personal and intimate, it may be helpful to think of it as a KISS:

- **K**neel before God. Prayer is a great opportunity to express your gratitude. As you acknowledge God's greatness, His love washes over you. You can kneel physically before Him or you can bow your heart before Him. Your posture is not as important as your motive. Whether you lie prostrate on the floor or look up to the sky, the position of your heart is what touches God's heart. He will hear the prayers of one that has a pure heart, whose motives are surrendered to His will.

- Invite God into your day. When you wake up in the morning, have a dialogue with your Lord. Acknowledge His mercy toward you. For instance, you could pray something like this, "I invite You into this day and give you full permission to be Lord over my life, my day, my goals, my plans, my dreams, my problems, my concerns, my meetings ... my everything."

- Self-evaluation is also an important part of prayer. God will speak and convict when you really value His truth. You can pray, *Lord, this is my situation. This is how I'm doing. I did some good things. Here they are. And I fell short in some areas. This is how I messed up. Here is what I should have done. Here is what I want to do. This is the result of my actions. Please forgive me, Lord. Thank You for Your grace, power, and forgiveness.*

- Supplication is the biblical term for taking your needs to the Lord. When you have needs and concerns, it is important to ask for God's help. You can also intercede on behalf of others. Intercession means that you are pleading with God for the needs of someone else. Praying for others is a great blessing. It strengthens your relationship with God as He grows your compassion for others. You may never truly know, until you get to Heaven, how your prayers moved the hand of God and brought blessings to the lives of others.

Psalm 46:10, BSB

"Be still and know that I am God."

After you come to God with your daily KISS, it's important not to abruptly end your time with Him. Leave space to wait and listen to God. You may say, "Lord, is there anything You want to talk to me about? Is there anything you want me to change? Is there anything you want me to stop doing? Is there a person you want me to pray for or bless in some way?" Scripture says that His sheep hear His voice. It may not be audible, but it will be unmistakable.

You may not be used to spending time with God. It may even be awkward for you. Even so, don't dismiss it. Satan will make every effort to thwart your effort to have a relationship with God. Don't listen to him. Don't let him trick you into being afraid to spend time in prayer. You don't have to be in a hurry. Just ask God to quiet your mind so His voice is the only one you hear.

Starting and ending your day in prayer activates God's peace and power in your life. Without talking to God in prayer, you are running on your own power. It can't sustain you. Only God's power can sustain you through the day and allow your night to be filled with peace.

Are you always in a hurry to get out of the house? Do you hit the snooze button and give yourself little time with God before running out to start your day? We've all been guilty of allowing distractions to keep us from praying. But God gives new mercies every day. Today or tomorrow can be your day to deepen your relationship with God by spending time with Him in prayer. Charles Spurgeon once said, "If your faith in Christ doesn't lead you to pray, have nothing to do with it, get rid of it, and ask God to help you begin again." Maybe it's time to ask God to help you begin again.

Prayer not only grows your relationship with God, but it also teaches you how to weather the storms of life. In fact, you may be in one right now. Are you looking for a way to make life better? Learn to pray. God helps you cope with the adversities in life. This is probably why the Bible talks more about prayer than most any other subject. Each verse can teach you something about the heart of God.

Jesus said, "The Scriptures declare, 'My temple will be called a house of prayer,' but you have turned it into a den of thieves" (Matthew 21:13, NLT). The people were doing things in the church that was never intended. Instead of praying to God, they were preying on people. How many churches do you know that are actually houses of prayer today? We have houses of worship, houses of teaching, houses that promote social justice and claim to know "what Jesus would do," but do we have houses of prayer? The number of churches today that could be considered houses of prayer are considerably few. That must sadden God.

1 John 5:14-15, NIV

This is the confidence we have in approaching God: that if we ask anything according to His will, He hears us. And if we know that He hears us—whatever we ask—we know that we have what we asked of Him.

This is one of the most powerful promises in the Bible. Think about the impact of what it says. We can ask God for anything and have confidence that He hears us and that we have what we ask for. However, this amazing promise is only true under one stipulation. If we ask anything, it must be *according to His will*. Treating God like a Santa Clause in the sky or a magic genie is useless. That is a false perception of who God is. He is your Heavenly Father, the Giver of every good gift. But He is more interested in developing your character than satisfying your every whim.

So, what about the prayers that God hasn't answered? Do you think they are definitely in His will? Did you give up and stop asking? Many of us have. The will and timing of God often look different than you might expect. Sometimes, God isn't saying, "No," to our prayers. Sometimes, He is simply saying, "Not yet." These "not yet" prayer answers are difficult. Our patience grows thin and our doubts make us wonder why God didn't answer.

There are many reasons that God may not answer our prayers as we think He should. Here are just a few:

- We are asking something that is not in the will of God.

- God has a better or different answer.

- God wants to change us or our situation before He answers our prayer. If we lack spiritual discernment or maturity, God may be trying to build our faith so we can be ready for the answer when it comes. He may want to develop qualities in us like discipline, trust, compassion, and submission.

Romans 8:28, NIV

And we know that in all things God works for the good of those who love him, who have been called according to his purpose.

This is a fallen world, and the consequences can have an adverse effect on innocent people. In situations where we prayed for God to move and He didn't, we must trust that He will still work it out for our good. This does not mean bad things are good. Instead, it means that we can trust God to bring good out of it. He is God and He is faithful. His ways are not our ways.

There are times when God answers prayers and we are shocked that He did so. We cannot predict God's miracles. Nevertheless, we shouldn't shrink back from asking God to move Heaven and Earth to answer our prayers. Expecting God to answer our prayers should be a given. Being at peace with how God answers, on the other hand, is a sign that we truly trust God. To repeat what Dr. Charles Stanley likes to say, "Obey God and leave the results to Him." Humanly speaking, this seems unnatural. That's because it truly is supernatural. If you are speaking and hearing God's heavenly language, you can trust His answers.

Your relationship with God should be your most important relationship. Prayer can make that a reality. With that in mind, consider the key passage for Anchor 10 and commit it to memory. It will serve you well.

1 Thessalonians 5:16-18, ESV

Be joyful always; pray continually; give thanks in all circumstances, for this is God's will for you in Christ Jesus.

When you spend daily time in prayer, joy and gratitude become natural byproducts. It would be impossible to spend time with your Father every day and not be joyful as a result. And there is only one way to find this out for yourself. Spend time with your Father and grow that relationship!

Ask Yourself

How often do I pray? What are my motives?

How does prayerful dialogue with God benefit my relationship with Him?

What obstacles keep me from praying more often?

What intentional things will I do to improve my prayer life so that I grow in my relationship with God?

How is God changing me when I pray?

What is God saying to me when I pray?

Write a personal KISS prayer to God. Imagine that God is standing right in front of you. Later, be willing to share your prayer with your group.

ANCHOR 11

GET DRESSED DAILY FOR BATTLE BY PUTTING ON GOD'S ARMOR AND TAKING MY THOUGHTS CAPTIVE.

Pray

As you begin this lesson, pray that you will have an Encounter with God as you earnestly seek Him. Don't rush through reading everything and don't rush through praying. Take some time to stop and listen so you may hear what God wants to say to you. Be sure to write whatever comes to your mind in your journal as you use the following as a prayer to the Lord:

Lord, I want to hear Your voice—and Your voice alone—through Your Word and throughout this lesson.

With every scripture or compilation of scriptures, pray these specific prayers:

Lord, what are You saying in Your Word?
Lord, what are You saying to me?
Lord, how do You want me to apply this to my life?

Journal everything that comes to your mind.

Therefore put on the full armor of God, so that when the day of evil comes, you may be able to stand your ground.

—Ephesians 6:13, NIV

The weapons we fight with are not the weapons of the world. On the contrary, they have divine power to demolish strongholds. We demolish arguments and every pretension that sets itself up against the knowledge of God, and we take captive every thought to make it obedient to Christ.

—2 Corinthians 10:4-5, NIV

PREPARE FOR BATTLE

A constant battle rages in the mind and affects every aspect of life. We only see our natural environment and are often unaware that we are surrounded by a spiritual world. There are forces of good and evil in the heavenly realms; angels and demons are not visible to the human eye. Many people tend to ignore what they cannot see or explain, but that is a huge mistake. The enemy should not be ignored or underestimated.

God loves you, but Satan hates you. God desires good for you. Satan desires to destroy and kill you. God is greater and more powerful than anything Satan can throw at you, but it would be naive to believe that Satan won't use every trick to convince you otherwise. His attacks may be big and relentless, but God is so much bigger. For this reason, it is vital to first focus on God's greatness. With this being in the forefront, we can be equipped with the wisdom, truth, awareness, and tools that God supplies in His Word. He doesn't want you to be a victim. He wants you to be victorious.

John 16:33, NIV

"I have told you these things, so that in Me you may have peace. In this world you will have trouble. But take heart! I have overcome the world."

You are going to have troubles. But the good news is that God is with you. He gives wisdom in His Word that can equip you. He helps through every battle. Even so, you still make the choice of how to respond. Will you allow God to help you win the battles in life?

God knows that you get weary in the process of fighting off the enemy's attacks. Life on earth can truly be brutal when you try to fight your battles in your own strength and power. God not only fights for His own, but He also instructs them on how to suit up for battle and defend themselves.

It all sounds like a good plan, doesn't it? Why, then, do we often get sucker punched by the devil as if God hadn't warned us or left us with a battle plan? It often comes down to unbelief. Satan is a deceiver, and people don't believe the truth of God. This leaves us vulnerable to attacks that have the potential to wreck our lives. It has always been Satan's plan to steal and kill and destroy us.

John 10:10, NIV

"The thief comes only to steal and kill and destroy; I have come that they may have life, and have it to the full."

Believing in Jesus and following His instructions is the key to resisting the ploys of the devil. Satan is the thief, but Jesus is the shepherd. Satan destroys, but Jesus protects. Satan lies, but Jesus is truth. Satan is death. Jesus is life.

Satan is a menace, but he does not have divine power. He cannot read your mind. Though he is cunning, he does not have access to your innermost thoughts. He does know, however, what makes you tick (and he knows what ticks you off). He studies your patterns, habits, coping mechanisms, and reactions. While he cannot access your thoughts, he can influence them. He puts subtle temptations before you as a way to derail you. He is the master of deceit.

Not even Jesus was exempt from the attacks of Satan. Why would you think he would not come after you too? Jesus resisted the devil by reminding him of God's Word. Because Jesus knew the Word and the truth, He was ultimately victorious.

Matthew 4:1-11, NIV

Then Jesus was led by the Spirit into the wilderness to be tempted by the devil. After fasting forty days and forty nights, he was hungry. The tempter came to him and said, "If you are the Son of God, tell these stones to become bread." Jesus answered, "It is written: 'Man shall not live on bread alone, but on every word that comes from the mouth of God.'" Then the devil took him to the holy city and had him stand on the highest point of the temple. "If you are the Son of God," he said, "throw yourself down. For it is written: 'He will command his angels concerning you, and they will lift you up in their hands, so that you will not strike your foot against a stone.'"

Jesus answered him, "It is also written: 'Do not put the Lord your God to the test.'" Again, the devil took him to a very high mountain and showed him all the kingdoms of the world and their splendor. "All this I will give you," he said, "if you will bow down and worship me." Jesus said to him, "Away from me, Satan! For it is written: 'Worship the Lord your God, and serve him only.'" Then the devil left him, and angels came and attended him.

Jesus had fasted for forty days. He was tired and hungry. Satan targeted Jesus in what he viewed as areas of weakness. He knew that if he could get Jesus to be tempted in some way, then he could accuse Him of failure. But the plan of God could not be thwarted. Jesus remained steadfast in the Father's love and truth. Jesus answered the distortions of Satan repeatedly with the words, "It is written." He quoted the Words of truth.

If you know God's Word, you can use it to resist the temptations of Satan. If you don't know God and His Word, you will be devoured. The enemy will set a trap that keeps you in a cycle of sin, condemnation, shame, and guilt.

I recently heard someone recounting the wisdom of an older lady he knew as a child. She would say, "Listen, young man, don't ever do anything that the devil could use as a stick to beat you up with." This lady had been around long enough to learn that, once you give in to temptation, he turns right back around to condemn. It's all part of his strategy to destroy your life.

Satan is at the root of much despair, discouragement, doubt, difficulty, discomfort, and darkness in this world. He attacks from every angle. He goes after you, your spouse, marriage, family, kids, job, reputation, character, contentment, peace, and happiness. The list is endless. He is often successful because he waits for just the right time when you are vulnerable to his tricks.

If you don't believe Satan can touch you, watch out. That is exactly what he wants you to think. Pride will tell you that there is no devil, or he wants nothing to do with your life. If that is what you believe, he has already deceived you. Because pride doesn't leave much room for God, he will attack a prideful person much more easily than a humble person. He's crafty that way.

You don't have to be obsessed with Satan; you just need to be aware of him. If knowing God is your greatest weapon against spiritual warfare, it would help to explore what He has said about it.

GOD ALONE IS GOD!

There really is no comparison between God and Satan. God is your Creator and Satan is one of His created beings who rebelled against God. This fallen world is a result of the sin and consequences caused by Satan. Nevertheless, God's Word says Satan is already defeated. The blood that Jesus shed on the cross conquered him. God also knows how the story ends. He has already appointed a day when Satan can no longer wreak havoc in this world. Satan also knows this. Therefore, he has pledged an all-out assault to keep as many people as possible from believing in God and spending eternity in Heaven with Him. This earth is his battlefield. That's the bad news. You were born in a battle. The good news, however, is that you were born to win.

1 John 4:4, BSB

Greater is He who is in you than he who is in the world.

Satan is not afraid of you, but he is afraid of who is in you. He is afraid of God's Holy Spirit.

Ephesians 6:12, NIV

For our struggle is not against flesh and blood, but against the rulers, against the authorities, against the powers of this dark world and against the spiritual forces of evil in the heavenly realms.

That sounds like a suspenseful fantasy novel, right? In some ways, it is a novel, and it's about you. God is the author of life, light, and good. Satan is the author of death, darkness, and evil. You can choose to be a product of goodness or a pawn of the enemy. Your story may have begun a bit shakily, and you may have experienced many trials and setbacks, but it's never too late to let God be the author and finisher of your faith.

It's important to know that spiritual warfare will happen. The devil truly wants to destroy you. He does not want you to have peace or to live for God. Indeed, followers of Christ are subject to persecution in this life. Satan does not want any of us to follow Jesus or overcome our problems. When he observes a true disciple of Jesus, he ramps up his efforts to derail them. He is relentless. **You can expect it.**

War was common in biblical times. Weapons were sharp and deadly. So, the soldier would cover his entire body with an external hard armor to protect himself. By doing so, he could deflect the weapons used against him in battle. A soldier would never dream of going into battle without his armor. Therefore, "getting dressed" for battle was vital to survival. Likewise, getting appropriately dressed by putting on your protective armor is vital to your survival.

Ephesians 6:10-18, NIV

Finally, be strong in the Lord and in his mighty power. Put on the full armor of God, so that you can take your stand against the devil's schemes. For our struggle is not against flesh and blood, but against the rulers, against the authorities, against the powers of this dark world and against the spiritual forces of evil in the heavenly realms. Therefore put on the full armor of God, so that when the day of evil comes, you may be able to stand your ground, and after you have done everything, to stand. Stand firm then, with the belt of truth buckled around your waist, with the breastplate of righteousness in place, and with your feet fitted with the readiness that comes from the gospel of peace. In addition to all this, take up the shield of faith, with which you can extinguish all the flaming arrows of the evil one. Take the helmet of salvation and the sword of the Spirit, which is the word of God.

And pray in the Spirit on all occasions with all kinds of prayers and requests. With this in mind, be alert and always keep on praying for all the Lord's people.

Paul instructs us as to how we can utilize every spiritual weapon God has placed at our disposal. Let's break each one down to see what it means to fully put on this armor:

- **Be strong** (v. 10). However, do not rely on your own strength. Lean on the strength of the Lord and His mighty power. That's Life Recovery 101. Stop trying to do what only God can do. Surrender to Him and allow Him to transform you.

- **Stand against the devil's schemes** (v. 11). You already know the devil is up to no good. When he attacks, you can be prepared. Take your stand according to God's Word.

- **Accept that there's a spiritual battle raging** (v. 12). Many are in denial that a spiritual world even exists, but God tells us that it does. Denying the existence of the devil won't make demons go away. It will only serve to defeat you. You cannot face your demons until you acknowledge that they do, in fact, exist. People are not your enemies.

Satan is your real enemy. Therefore, your real battles are not against flesh and blood (i.e., real people), but against the rulers, authorities, and powers of this dark world. You may have been exhausting your efforts in fighting the wrong target. You shouldn't blame people or God when trouble hits. Blame the one who really is your enemy, Satan. If you are going to get mad at anyone, get mad at him. He is the author of any chaos associated with your life.

- **Put on the full armor of God** (v. 13). You are vulnerable to the enemy's attacks. You must purposefully pray and daily apply God's armor over your life. This helps you stand your ground so you can win.

- **Put on the belt of truth around your waist** (v. 14). Know God and His Word. Make truth the authority over your life. This belt will allow you to exercise godly integrity at all times and in all situations.

- **Put on the breastplate of righteousness** (v. 14). Righteousness is one of the attributes of God. It is everything good, right, and holy. It represents purity of heart, of always keeping your motives clean and pure. Satan likes to attack your heart where you have deep-seated emotions. The sacrifice of Jesus on the cross made it possible for believers to put on His perfect righteousness in place of their own limited righteousness. He exchanged your sin for His righteousness. He wore your sin so you could wear His righteousness. Satan likes to attack your purity and he will use pornography, movies, books, songs, anything he can to keep your heart from being pure. When you are clothed in the righteousness of Christ, your heart is guarded to help you resist temptation. The very blood of Jesus is your protection.

- **Put on the shoes of peace** (v. 15). Share the good news of Christ. The gospel is a message of peace, and believers are called to live it out daily by telling others.

Anchor 11

- **Take up the shield of faith** (v. 16). A shield is a defensive weapon. Satan is constantly shooting his flaming arrows at you. You can extinguish them through faith. Taking up the shield of faith can guard you against Satan's fiery darts of doubt, denial, and deceit.

- **Wear the helmet of salvation** (v. 17). A helmet protects your head, your mind. If your head is wounded in a battle, it is a fatal blow. The helmet of salvation protects your mind from evil thoughts. Satan wants you to doubt God. Salvation, through the blood of Jesus Christ, gives you a new mind. This new mind protects you from evil. Satan will try to impact your thoughts by any means possible (e.g., television, books, music). He will use anything to distort your thinking. Instead, you must guard your mind with the helmet of salvation

- **Take the sword of the Spirit** (v. 17). The sword is God's Word and Holy Spirit living within you. The more you are led by the Holy Spirit, through God's Word, the more equipped you become to withstand the temptations of the enemy. Using your sword is going on the offensive against Satan. It enables you to recognize truth from error. With the sword, you can put Satan on notice. As Jesus did, you can say with confidence, "It is written." You can recognize when and how the devil is twisting or distorting God's truth, so you can say, "Get behind me, Satan" (Matthew 16:23). He has to get behind the Holy Spirit of God living inside of you. The blood of Jesus has covered your sins and already defeated Satan.

- **Pray in the Spirit with all kinds of intercession** (v. 18). To those who do not know what it means, praying in the Spirit doesn't have to be confusing or scary. The Holy Spirit of God leads you into truth. The Holy Spirit of God points you to Jesus. The Holy Spirit of God knows what you should do and how you should pray. You can trust His guidance. Pray as He directs. Be discerning. He knows how to win the battles. Pray that you may be able to yield accordingly and be led into victory.

Following this great battle plan can be the difference between living in victory and suffering defeat. Whether it is your past, present, or future, the only way to recover is to follow God's design for triumph.

BECOMING AN EXPERT AT TAKING THOUGHTS CAPTIVE

2 Corinthians 10:3-5, NIV

For though we live in the world, we do not wage war as the world does. The weapons we fight with are not the weapons of the world. On the contrary, they have divine power to demolish strongholds. We demolish arguments and every pretension that sets itself up against the knowledge of God, and we take captive every thought to make it obedient to Christ.

This shows, once again, there truly is a battle raging between good and evil. Satan will do anything to make you reject the truth of God and believe his lies. However, the weapons followers of Christ have in their arsenal are mighty. They are not natural weapons; God's divine power gives you the power to demolish strongholds with them. So, don't walk around in defeat with your head hung low. You can activate the divine power of God in your life to overcome the strongholds that afflict you.

Paul instructs believers on how to do this. "Take captive every thought," he says, "to make it obedient to Christ." In other words, God gives the wisdom, discernment, and power to recognize the lies of the enemy and speak His truth against them.

When you take something captive, you take possession of it. You stop allowing it to control you. In fact, you take control of it. You don't have to believe the lies of Satan or others. You can yield to the truth of God's Word. The power of His Holy Spirit can help you discern what is really going on. It gives you the ability to say, "Not today,

Satan!" Whenever you have an ungodly thought or a temptation that opposes God, you have the ability to take that thought captive to the obedience of Jesus Christ. You don't have to give in. In the heat of battle, you can pray something like this, "Is this of You, God? Is this good? Does this line up with what I know to be true of You? Help me to surrender to Your ways."

When you utilize your heavenly arsenal by taking every thought captive, you will start to experience victory over strongholds. You will start to recognize the lies of the enemy and speak the truth of God. You will no longer be a hostage to the temptations of Satan. Instead, you will readily allow God to make you strong enough to reject those temptations and surrender them to Him.

Though we have thought at length about spiritual warfare, it is important not to look for a demon around every corner or beneath every rock. Be aware of the real war Satan has waged against you but remember that God is greater. He has given you the provision to defeat the enemy's lies. God has given you everything you need to have victory in this life. Look to Him and trust in Him. Yield your battles to Him, but be ready to get in the fight.

James 4:6-7, ESV

God opposes the proud but gives grace to the humble. Submit yourselves then to God. Resist the devil, and he will flee from you.

The following equation summarizes how we fight. When faced with a temptation, think of it in this way:

Humble + Submit + Resist = He Will Flee

As you humble and submit yourself to God in every area of your life, you will have greater power to resist the enemy. He will flee from you, in Jesus's name.

Ask Yourself

What is an example of spiritual warfare in my life? How can getting dressed daily for battle guard me against Satan's lies and help me resist temptation?

What keeps me from applying God's Word to my thought life?

What thoughts do I need to take captive to the obedience of Christ?

Everyone gets dressed before leaving their house. In the same way, God's armor is your covering of protection each day. With this in mind, write your own prayer and battle plan based on Ephesians 6:10-18. Afterward, share it with your group or a trusted individual.

⚓ Anchor 12

LIVE OUT AND SHARE THE HOPE THAT I NOW HAVE.

Pray

As you begin this lesson, pray that you will have an Encounter with God as you earnestly seek Him. Don't rush through reading everything and don't rush through praying. Take some time to stop and listen so you may hear what God wants to say to you. Be sure to write whatever comes to your mind in your journal as you use the following as a prayer to the Lord:

Lord, I want to hear Your voice—and Your voice alone—through Your Word and throughout this lesson.

With every scripture or compilation of scriptures, pray these specific prayers:

Lord, what are You saying in Your Word?
Lord, what are You saying to me?
Lord, how do You want me to apply this to my life?

Journal everything that comes to your mind.

Always be prepared to give an answer to everyone who asks you to give the reason for the hope that you have.

—1 Peter 3:15, NIV

WHAT WILL YOUR ANSWER BE?

Hope has changed us. And because of the transformation we have experienced, we must share hope with others.

We know that, to truly recover from any adversity or hurt in life, we must come to know God and His Word. As we become Christ followers, we learn to live gratefully toward God. Gratitude and surrender allow God to transform our minds and hearts. Afterward, our thoughts and actions begin to line up with the new nature God has given us.

This not only changes our eternal destiny, it changes the rest of life here on earth. God can help us recover from any adversity. As we grow in wisdom, truth, and character, we begin to discover that we have choices in life. We learn that God can help us respond in better and healthier ways to adversity. As we begin to recover from the things that have hurt us or caused brokenness, we find that others are also finding hope in Christ. We discover that being accountable to God and sharing life with others is a big part of getting better.

Sharing our struggles, celebrations, and hope in a safe community can bring great healing in our lives. Once we have tasted and seen that the Lord is good, our gratitude compels us to want to tell the world about Him. We want others to encounter God and have the kind of life-changing experience we have had.

Evangelism involves telling others God's story through sharing our own story of transformation. When we spread the gospel, the easiest way for others to know that it is real is to see how it has changed us. When we are truly transformed by God, our life reflects those changes. People will take notice and start asking questions. We must be ready to answer.

Anchor 12

Christ is the anchor for our soul. He is our hope. When we share that with others, we bring God glory and help them find hope. How, then, can we best share that message?

The most effective way to evangelize starts by looking at Jesus's example. The recurring theme of His ministry could be paraphrased as, "Come and see, follow Me, then go and tell." As Jesus ministered to others, He invited them to hear the truth of the gospel and to follow Him. Later, He instructed them to tell others what they had learned and experienced. That same invitation is ours today.

By applying the 12 Anchors to our life, we are living out the principles of, "Come and see, follow Me, then go and tell." Jesus invites us all to come and see what life with Him is all about. Come and see what grace is. Come and see what forgiveness is. Come and see what eternal life is. Come and see what salvation is. Come experience healing. Come experience freedom.

Once we taste and see the greatness of the Lord, He invites us to follow Him. He invites us to die to our old selves and follow His ways. He knows it won't be easy or popular; this is why He sent the Holy Spirit to help us. He invites us to let go of the grip of this earthly life so we can grab hold of the eternal life He has for us in Heaven. He invites us to crucify our old selves, our selfish desires, our human instincts, our earthly ambitions, our past, and anything else that would keep us from the ways of Jesus.

James 4:4, NIV

You adulterous people, don't you know that friendship with the world means enmity against God? Therefore, anyone who chooses to be a friend of the world becomes an enemy of God.

Our choices matter both for today and for eternity. When Jesus invites us to follow Him, it is an all-inclusive invitation. His arms are open wide. He wants all of us all of the time. Why does He want all of us? Because it is God's best plan for our life and our ultimate good. He wants us to go all -in with Him because it is the only way to experience freedom in this life. His ways are indeed higher than our ways. Trust that His ways are better.

Finally, Jesus invites us to go and tell. Jesus gives more than just an invitation to follow Him. Later, He gives a command to go and tell others the good news of Jesus Christ. God doesn't give us an option. He doesn't say to do it only if we feel comfortable doing so. He commands that we go and tell the world about Him. It is known as The Great Commission.

Matthew 28:18-20, NIV

Then Jesus came to them and said, "All authority in heaven and on earth has been given to me. Therefore go and make disciples of all nations, baptizing them in the name of the Father and of the Son and of the Holy Spirit, and teaching them to obey everything I have commanded you. And surely I am with you always, to the very end of the age."

By telling others about the saving work of Jesus, we spread the good news and give away to others what was given to us. We have found the cure, the antidote to living a life destined for Hell. We know that only Jesus offers the salvation that forgives. Now, we get to tell others about Him. We can invite them to come and see. We can call them to follow. And, as they do, we can commission them to go and tell. God has allowed us to be a part of spreading the gospel so others can know Him and be in Heaven. The goal is to take as many people to Heaven with us as possible.

LIVING OUT THE GREAT COMMISSION

Philippians 2:1-11, NIV

Therefore if you have any encouragement from being united with Christ, if any comfort from his love, if any common sharing in the Spirit, if any tenderness and compassion, then make my joy complete by being like-minded, having the same love, being one in spirit and of one mind. Do nothing out of selfish ambition or vain conceit. Rather, in humility value others above yourselves, not looking to your own interests but each of you to the interests of the others. In your relationships with one another, have the same mindset as Christ Jesus: Who, being in very nature God, did not consider equality with God something to be used to his own advantage; rather, he made himself nothing by taking the very nature of a servant, being made in human likeness. And being found in appearance as a man, he humbled himself by becoming obedient to death—even death on a cross! Therefore God exalted him to the highest place and gave him the name that is above every name, that at the name of Jesus every knee should bow, in heaven and on earth and under the earth, and every tongue acknowledge that Jesus Christ is Lord, to the glory of God the Father.

When we live out the Great Commission, we serve others freely. We do nothing out of selfish ambition or vain conceit, but in humility consider others better than ourselves. We help others less fortunate. We walk alongside someone who is struggling with pain or hurt. We give to others with an attitude of gratitude. We are thankful and filled with hope. We open our hearts, wallets, and lives to support God's agenda.

Acts 20:24, NLT

But my life is worth nothing to me unless I use it for finishing the work assigned to me by the Lord Jesus—the work of telling others the good news about the wonderful grace of God.

When we go and tell, we may be the only Bible someone will ever hear. We must make sure we are a good translation. One that is grace-filled, humble, and led by the Holy Spirit.

Matthew 10:32-33, NLT

"Everyone who acknowledges Me [Jesus] publicly here on earth, I will also acknowledge before My Father in heaven. But everyone who denies Me here on earth, I will also deny before My Father in heaven."

Encounter

Jesus's ministry and death were public. He died for all the world to see. He wants our faith to also be public. He wants our hope to be loud.

Ephesians 2:10, NKJV

For we are His workmanship, created in Christ Jesus for good works, which God prepared beforehand that we should walk in them.

We are God's workmanship, His masterpiece. We were created to go public with the gifts that God gave and the mission He planned. Whether we realize it or not, we are giving answers to a world that has questions. The way we live communicates the hope for which we live. People around us are watching. Are we emulating a life that has hope? Do we love and live like Jesus? Are our lives led by the Holy Spirit?

People don't care so much about what we know. They want to see if we are willing to live out our convictions. People want to see how we handle adversities, setbacks, and disappointments. They want to see what our answers are for the hope in the midst of it all. What kind of answers are we giving?

Encounter's 12 Anchors of Hope will help give an answer for the hope we now have. If we learn what God is all about, it will give an answer. If we follow Jesus, it will give an answer. If we go and tell others what He has done for us, it will give an answer.

Here are some practical ways we can tell others of the hope we now have:

- Love and serve God and others.
- Be spiritual leaders for our family.
- Volunteer to help with local church ministries and encourage the body of Christ.
- Give generously of our time, talents, and finances to God and others.
- Live humbly for God's glory and not for our own selfish desires.
- Share how we came to faith in Jesus Christ.

We have many examples of this type of living in Scripture. The Apostle Paul said, "For me, to live is Christ and to die is gain" (Philippians 1:21, CSB). He wanted to die to himself. He wanted to deny his selfish sinful nature and live out the purposes of God. He wanted others to encounter Jesus and be transformed as he had been. He lived to go and tell.

In the same way, John the Baptist said, "He must increase, but I must decrease" (John 3:30, ESV). John had been transformed by the power of God. Because of that, his desire was to let others see Christ in and through his life. When we have the best news in the world, we want to share it.

Even Jesus made Himself nothing to accomplish the purposes and plan of the Father. He came to serve rather than to be served. He humbled Himself repeatedly. He came in the form of a baby. He suffered and died to take the sins of the world upon Himself. He was obedient to God the Father, all the way to death. (Philippians 2:1-11)

If you have applied the 12 Anchors to your life, you will never be the same. You are already different than when you first started this study. You've made many important decisions:

You decided to get well and admitted that you do a terrible job at playing God.

You made the decision to accept God's love through His Son and trust the finished work of Christ. You now have hope and a firm foundation.

You trusted in the power of the Holy Spirit to lead and guide you.

You found a new identity in Christ.

You got honest about the past and allowed God to reveal the root issues in your life.

You committed to becoming a disciple by allowing God to transform your life.

You closed all your accounts with others by forgiving them and experienced the peace of God.

You submitted to God's Word as the authority over your life.

You made prayer a priority to grow your relationship with Christ.

You readied yourself for spiritual battles by getting dressed in the armor of God, learning how to take thoughts captive to the obedience of Christ.

And, as a result of living out all these Anchors of Hope, your mission in life is now to share them in word and deed!

1 Peter 3:15, NIV

But in your hearts revere Christ as Lord. Always be prepared to give an answer to everyone who asks you to give the reason for the hope that you have.

Not every person who comes to faith is called to preach, but we are all commissioned to go and share the hope we now have. Our words should represent a life well lived. Be a good translation so people can appropriately interpret the hope you now have.

Some of the best sermons I have ever heard did not come from pastors in the pulpit. They came from ordinary people who share their stories of faith. That gives people hope because they realize that *if God can do that for them, He can do it for me.*

In the end, there's always a choice. We can choose to be selfish, or we can choose to be a servant. We can either ask, "What's in it for me?" or "How can I share this good news with others?" Overcomers share their hope and healing. Because we now know where hope can be found, we invite everyone to come and see, follow Jesus, then go and tell others about Him.

Here is a thought for you to ponder. One hundred years from now the only thing that will matter is who is in Heaven and who is not.

Who in your world do you want to spend eternity in Heaven with you?

Ask Yourself

What holds me back from serving, giving, and sharing the hope that I now have? What part of my life am I holding onto with clenched fists?

Read Acts 20:24, NLT once again. "But my life is worth nothing to me unless I use it for finishing the work assigned me by the Lord Jesus—the work of telling others the good news about the wonderful grace of God."

The Apostle Paul knew the importance of his assignment. Ask God: What is my ministry assignment? Where do You want me to serve in order to share my hope with others? How do You want me to make disciples? How have You gifted me to go and tell?

Compared to when I first started this study, what is different about me now? How do I handle adversity differently? What healing and changes have I experienced? What root issues did God expose and heal in my life?

Write and share a short testimony of your life. In it, recount your past and the significant events that shaped your life. Describe how you found hope by surrendering your life to Jesus Christ. End by explaining the work God has done since coming to faith.

AFTERWORD

When we become a follower of Jesus, we are not left to live the Christian life alone. The ministry of Encounter was formed to help people know where hope can be found in the face of life's adversities. Our signature verse is Hebrews 6:19, NIV, "We have this hope as an anchor for the soul, firm and secure."

We are honored that you have given the time and effort to work through the Encounter Study. Our prayer is that God has transformed your life and that you have embraced all you have learned and found true hope in Him. Remember, you can continue to live as an overcomer who glorifies God in everything you say and do. The joy of the Lord will be your strength.

Philippians 2:14-18, NIV

Do everything without grumbling or arguing, so that you may become blameless and pure, children of God, without fault in a warped and crooked generation. **Then you will shine among them like stars in the sky as you hold firmly to the Word of life.** And then I will be able to boast on the day of Christ that I did not run or labor in vain. But even if I am being poured out like a drink offering on the sacrifice and service coming from your faith, I am glad and rejoice with all of you. So you too should be glad and rejoice with me. (emphasis added)

God is faithful. Keep your eyes, mind, and heart on Him. He is with you, and He will keep you. Be well and live well as you go and tell. Shine among them like stars in the sky!

About Encounter

Encounter is a life recovery and discipleship ministry based on the 12 Anchors of Hope. Through its personal study and application as well as weekly meetings, participants learn that it is possible to have an authentic encounter with God. The Scriptures and principles found in God's Word provide hope in, through, and despite the adversities of life.

To learn more or to start an Encounter Study in your area, visit TheHopeEncounter.org.

But **my life** is *worth nothing* to me
unless I use it for **finishing the work**
assigned me by the **Lord Jesus**—the
work of **telling others the Good News**
about the **wonderful grace** of **God**.

—Acts 20:24, NLT

ABOUT THE AUTHOR

Bill and Carolynn Rieser have learned that having joyful freedom in this life comes only through a committed and surrendered walk with Jesus Christ as their Lord and Savior. For them, there is no other path to break the chains of addiction and pain that come from adversities in life. They have observed that people can't change themselves, but they can allow God to transform their way of thinking and coping.

Bill's faith journey began with a complete and sincere life conversion in his late thirties. Bill's was a road-to-Damascus kind of conversion, much like the Apostle Paul's. Not unlike Paul, Bill's only response was, "Lord, who are you and what would you have me to do?". Bill's former life had been ruled by his sinful lifestyle. That all turned around with one amazing Encounter with the living God. Bill invited Jesus to be his Lord and Savior, and the Holy Spirit came to be his guide. Bill has been all-in with following Jesus ever since God's grace saved him.

Made in the USA
Monee, IL
03 November 2023

45703230R00095